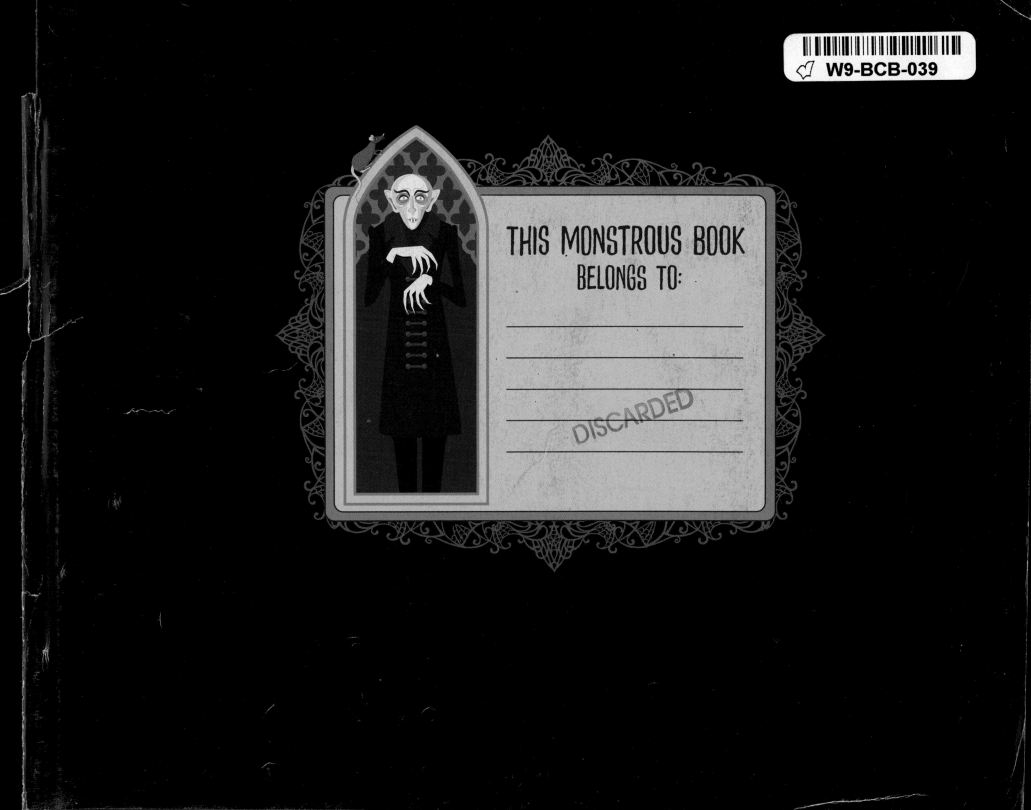

THIS MONSTROUS BOOK
BELONGS TO:

_____

_____

_____

DISCARDED

_____

TO MY FATHER AND HIS TERRIFYING TALES OF GOGA

Carolrhoda Books®
An imprint of Lerner Publishing Group, Inc.
241 First Avenue North
Minneapolis, MN 55401 USA

For reading levels and more information, look up this title at

Designed by Carlyn Beccia and Danielle Carnito.
Main body text set in ITC Franklin Gothic.
Typeface provided by Adobe Systems.
The illustrations in this book were created with mixed media.

Library of Congress Cataloging-in-Publication Data

The Cataloging-in-Publication Data for *Monstrous: The Lore, Gore, and Science behind Your Favorite Monsters* is on file at the Library of Congress.
ISBN 978-1-5124-4916-7 (lib. bdg.)
ISBN 978-1-5415-6260-8 (eb pdf)

LC record available at https://lccn.loc.gov/2019002795

Manufactured in the United States of America
1-42848-26512-5/16/2019

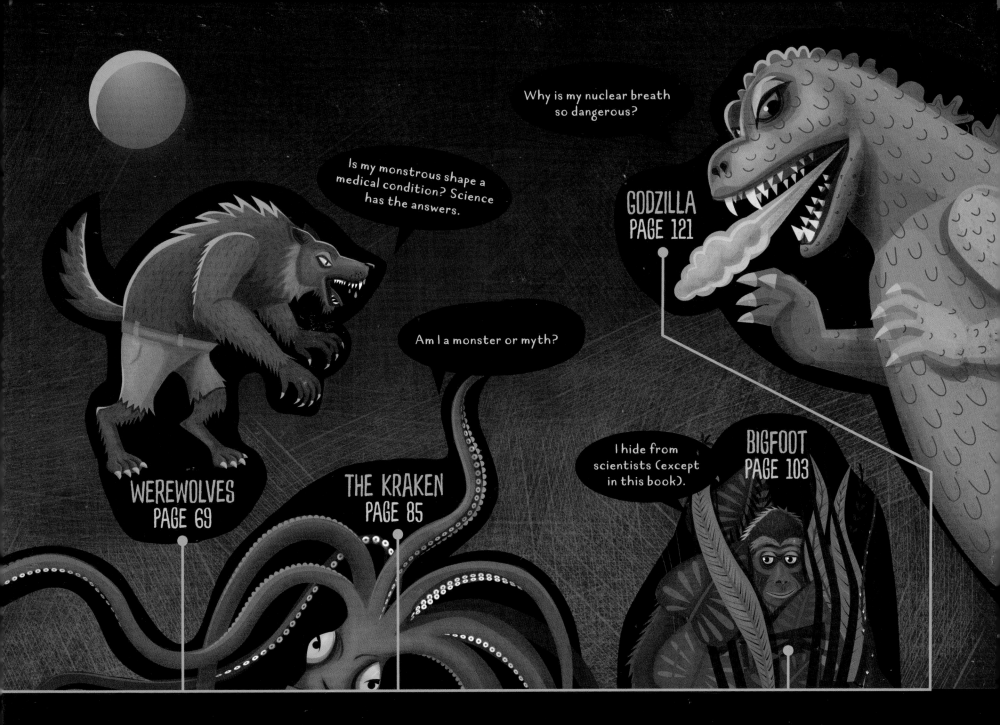

Why is my nuclear breath so dangerous?

Is my monstrous shape a medical condition? Science has the answers.

GODZILLA
PAGE 121

Am I a monster or myth?

I hide from scientists (except in this book).

BIGFOOT
PAGE 103

WEREWOLVES
PAGE 69

THE KRAKEN
PAGE 85

WHEN SCIENCE IS WRONG . . .
PAGE 140

SOURCE NOTES
PAGE 141

SELECTED BIBLIOGRAPHY
PAGE 142

GLOSSARY
PAGE 146

INDEX
PAGE 148

INTRODUCTION: THE MAGIC OF SCIENCE

In the fifth century, English ruler Vortigern was attempting to build a great fortress in Wales. But every time the foundation stones were laid, the ground shook and the fortress collapsed. When Vortigern consulted his wise advisors, they told him the fortress would never stand because the land was cursed. The only way to break the curse was to soak the foundation with the blood of a fatherless boy. They found such a boy in a nearby village, and the boy was brought before the king.

Upon learning that he was about to be human fertilizer, the boy insisted the real problem was not a curse on the land but, instead, two dragons: one red and one white. He said the dragons were trapped under the earth, and their fighting caused the ground to shake. Vortigern didn't need blood. He just needed to release the dragons.

So the king ordered the earth dug up, and he found the dragons in "hollow stones" and released them. Thereafter, the fortress stood strong. The king fired his advisors and made the boy his right-hand man. This boy grew up to become the great wizard, Merlin.

Was Merlin really a powerful wizard? Probably not. But perhaps he did know something about science. Wales is known for having pockets of the gas hydrogen sulfide trapped underground. Hydrogen sulfide has a pretty horrible, rotten-egg smell, and Merlin might have smelled it wafting through the air. Sometimes hydrogen sulfide mixes with the odorless gas, methane, and when these gases get trapped in rocks . . . *boom!* Explosions happen.

Merlin was clever. He knew he wasn't going to convince King Vortigern that his fears were not real so, instead, he used science to save himself. You too can use science to conquer monsters (and blame it on wizardry).

The monstrous have no magic. **The real magic is science.**

THE SCIENCE OF THE MONSTROUS

Millions of years ago, your prehistoric ancestors roamed the open plains. There were kids just like you. They picked berries, danced, and drew pretty pictures on caves. They had a blast hanging out at the local watering hole. You might even know some people like that today—always smiling and never scared or anxious about anything. You know . . . fearless people.

Yeah, those people died. Probably eaten by a saber-toothed tiger or bludgeoned to death by rivals while they were peacefully sleeping. But that apprehensive cavewoman with her spear at the ready, suspicious of every berry, and with one eye open as she slept . . . she survived. She is your great-great-great-grandmother (and probably a few more greats), and she has passed down her lessons of survival into the most primitive parts of your brain—fear keeps us alive.

The part of your brain that responds to fear has not changed since your prehistoric grandmother. When you are scared, an almond-shaped mass called the **amygdala (A)** activates a split-second

Your ancestor who did survive

Your ancestor who didn't survive

response called **fight-or-flight**. The fight-or-flight response causes your eyes to widen and pulse to quicken. It sends blood away from your intestines to your muscles so that you can either outrun the monster or stab it in the eye.

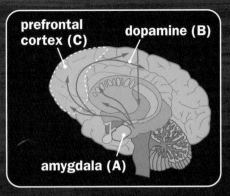

prefrontal cortex (C) dopamine (B)

amygdala (A)

During this process, the neurotransmitter **dopamine (B)** is released. Neurotransmitters are the messengers in your brain that tell you how to feel, but they are not always clear on which emotion. Have you ever noticed that when someone sneaks up behind you and screams, "Boo!" your first reaction is to startle, but your second reaction is often to laugh. (Possibly followed by plots of revenge against whomever scared you.) That is dopamine messing with your brain. Dopamine is released when you feel fear, but it is also released when you feel pleasure. This is partly why we enjoy fear. When we conquer our fear, it gives us a huge sense of accomplishment. Something has scared us, but we have survived.

Unfortunately, there is a downside to fear. Some people use fear to control the behavior of others. For example, I could convince you that a zombie apocalypse is coming and that you must read this book to survive. Then I would make tons of money, buy a castle in Spain, and live alone with my one-eyed cat and piles of Spam while you would fear every stranger as a possible zombie contaminate.

But I am going to do the opposite because I know you are too smart to be manipulated by fear. (And I already have a one-eyed cat, piles of Spam, and a castle in Spain.) Instead, I am going to activate your **prefrontal cortex (C)**. That's the part of your brain that controls reasoning, and it kicks in once your fight-or-flight response has calmed down. Your prefrontal cortex says, "Wait just a minute, Spam-hoarding lady with the one-eyed cat. I am not buying that 'vampires are going to suck my blood' nonsense because blood contains a very lethal mineral" (p. 34). And "Yes, the water is dark and scary, but the kraken just wants to be left alone to play with his kraken friends" (p. 85). And "Sorry, know-it-all author, but everyone knows zombies can't survive on a diet of brains because a brain is the least nutritious part of the human body" (p. 50). Why? Because of science. **Science is stronger than fear.**

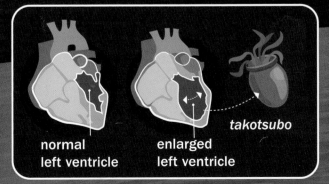

normal left ventricle

enlarged left ventricle

takotsubo

WHY YOU SHOULD NEVER STRESS YOUR MOM OUT

Your brain is not the only organ altered by fear. Under extreme stress, your heart's left ventricle can enlarge at the bottom and narrow at the top, like a balloon animal being tied off. Known as **takotsubo cardiomyopathy**, or "broken heart syndrome," the condition is named after a *takotsubo*—a Japanese pot used to trap octopuses. Far more women than men experience the condition, but fortunately, most people who have it recover.

FRANKENSTEIN'S MONSTER

You probably already know a little about Frankenstein: a wacky scientist steals body parts from local graves and cobbles them together to create a monster with a gigantic forehead and no eyebrows. He then brings the creature to life with a few electric jolts, and—voilà—a monster is born.

Let's start with what gave Frankenstein's creation the first sparks of life. Throughout the eighteenth and nineteenth centuries, a new science called an Entertainment for Angels was sweeping across Europe and North America. We know it today as electricity, but before light bulbs and televisions, no one really understood what this strange force of nature actually was. Was electricity a vapor, a fluid, or a supernatural fire?

WHAT IS ELECTRICITY?

Electricity begins with tiny units of matter too small to see without a microscope called **atoms**. Inside an atom is a **nucleus**. The nucleus contains **protons** with a positive charge and **neutrons** with no charge. Orbiting around the nucleus are negatively charged **electrons**. Atoms balance the positive charge of their protons with the negative charge of their electrons. But sometimes electrons break free and move to another atom. When this happens, one material ends up with too many electrons and becomes negatively charged, while the other ends up with too few electrons and becomes positively charged. This imbalance is electricity.

There are two main types of electricity—**static electricity** and **electric current**. When electricity builds up on a surface, it causes static electricity. You experience static electricity when you go down a slide. The slide transfers a positive charge to your hair, and because a positive charge repels another positive charge, your strands of hair stand on end to get away from one another. When electricity moves from one place to another, it is called an electric current. Examples of electric currents are light bulbs, batteries, motors or, in this case, Dr. Frankenstein's machine.

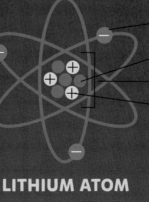

ELECTRONS

NEUTRONS

NUCLEUS

PROTONS

LITHIUM ATOM

No one in the eighteenth century understood how electric currents worked, but they did know one thing—electricity could be loads of fun. Scientists of the day held "electrical parties" in darkened rooms where they used "electrical machines" to crank out sparks that would make a lady's hair stand on end or turn a boy into a human static electricity generator. In the experiment called the flying boy, a boy was suspended from the ceiling by silk cords while a rotating sulfur ball charged his body with static electricity. The boy would then mysteriously pull tiny pieces of feathers and gold leaf onto his charged hands like a puppeteer making objects dance without strings.

It kind of freaked people out. It also proved the human body could conduct electricity and made people wonder whether electricity could reanimate the dead.

Italian scientist Luigi Galvani certainly thought so. In 1771, Galvani was dissecting a frog near an electrical generator when he noticed something strange. When two different pieces of metal touched a frog's nerve and its spinal cord at the same time, the leg muscle contracted. He used these experiments to hypothesize that all living beings have "animal electricity"—an electric fluid responsible for muscle contractions.

STATIC ELECTRICITY: THE FLYING BOY
In the flying boy experiment, a man cranked a sulfur ball (A), which transferred an electric charge to the boy (B) so that he could attract the oppositely charged feathers and gold leaf (C). To eighteenth-century audiences not familiar with static electricity,

ELECTRIC CURRENT: THE FROG BATTERY
Galvani believed living things contained a vital force called animal electricity. The electricity really came from the metals used to create a circuit, not from inside the frog's tissue. Today we understand that neurons, the heart, and muscle tissues all respond to outside

THE REAL CORPSE REANIMATOR

Now, making frog legs twitch was clearly entertaining, but Galvani's nephew, Giovanni Aldini, wanted to take his uncle's experiments one step further. He wanted to reanimate humans instead of amphibians. All he needed was a dead person to bring back to life. So Aldini convinced London officials to hand over the very dead corpse of a convicted murderer named George Forster so he could test his hypothesis.

In January of 1803, George Forster's corpse was laid out on a cold slab in a dimly lit basement before an eager crowd. Aldini attached electrodes to Forster's head, neck, chest, limbs, and . . . yes, even up his derrière. To these electrodes, he attached galvanic cells consisting of two oppositely charged metal plates immersed in tubes of acid.

As soon as the electric current entered Forster's lifeless body, one of his eyes flickered open. His face grimaced in agony. His fingers twitched. His back arched in protest, and his chest heaved up and down. Up and down. Faster and faster. And then, just as suddenly, the body lay motionless. Frustrated, Aldini cracked open Forster's sternum and applied the current to his heart, but the shriveled organ would not beat.

Aldini didn't bring Forster back to life, but he succeeded in making lifeless limbs twitch. At the very least, Forster did *seem* to come back to life for a few brief moments. And that terrified people. One man in the audience was so frightened, he died of shock later that night. Aldini went on to publish accounts of his electrical experiment on Forster, and it became the talk of Europe and America. Many people wondered—could the dead be brought back to life with electricity?

THE SUMMER OF DARKNESS

In the spring of 1815, Mount Tambora in present-day Indonesia awoke from her slumber. The volcano's eruption blanketed much of the globe with toxic ash, freezing rains, and a smoky haze that blotted out the sun. By 1816 the effects had reached even the distant shores of Geneva, Switzerland, where the days became so cold, dark, and gloomy, the period became known as the Year without a Summer.

Inside a tiny chalet in Geneva, a nineteen-year-old young lady was cooped up with her brooding friends because of the bad weather. Her name was Mary Wollstonecraft Godwin, and her companions were her future husband Percy Shelley, Dr. John Polidori, Claire Clairmont, and the notorious Lord George Gordon Byron. Lord Byron was known throughout Europe as the heartthrob author of his day with every young lady swooning over his poetry and novels.

On this particular night, Byron was bored. Byron didn't like to be bored. So he suggested a challenge . . . a ghost story challenge. Who amongst their group could write the scariest, most bloodcurdling tale?

I am bored.

Castle Frankenstein, in Germany, was once home to alchemist and scientist Johann Konrad Dippel. Dippel was rumored to steal bodies from the local graveyard and then try to reanimate them with various potions. It is unknown if Mary Shelley was inspired by these tales.

At the time, no one expected a young lady to accomplish such a feat, but Mary Shelley was not some blushing Romantic. That summer she crafted a horrific tale about a scientist named Victor Frankenstein who creates "a creature" from stolen body parts and brings his monster's dull, yellow eyes to life through electricity. The monster later turns on his creator, even killing Frankenstein's brother and young bride.

Mary didn't pull this story out of thin air. Like most people of her day, she had heard tales of Giovanni Aldini reanimating the dead and may have attended electrical parties. Her future husband, Percy, was so fascinated by electricity that he had his own electrical machine, which he would pull from the clutter of his desk to show friends how he could make sparks crackle.

Mary Shelley published her story anonymously in 1818 under the title *The Modern Prometheus*, but it would later be retitled *Frankenstein* and go on to sell millions of copies. In 1931, Universal Studios adapted the novel as the horror film *Frankenstein*. Over forty adaptations have been produced, but it was actor Boris Karloff in the 1931 version who became the iconic Frankenstein.

Mary Shelley originally set out to write a really scary ghost story, but she ended up with a novel that explored the consequences of science. Was science powerful enough to give life? And if it was, what price would we pay? Scientists today grapple with these questions every time they assemble humanoid robots, modify genes to make better **species**, or create more dangerous weapons.

SCIENCE VS. MONSTERS:
COULD DR. FRANKENSTEIN'S MACHINE EVER WORK?

It's alive!

In the 1931 movie, the monster lies on a raised operating table as flashes of lightning crash from above and electricity is directed through his body. The camera zooms in on the monster's quivering fingers as he lifts his arm up and the excited doctor cries, "It's alive! It's alive!" It's a dramatic scene, but could electricity ever truly create life? To answer that question, let's look at the science behind the mad doctor's machine.

To bring his creation to life, Dr. Frankenstein's first task is to direct an electric current into the monster. To create an electric current, scientists often use metals like aluminum and copper because they easily lose or gain electrons. These materials are called **conductors** because they conduct electricity. Materials like wood or rubber hold onto their electrons. These materials are called **insulators** because they do not conduct electricity. To conduct an electric current through the body, the doctor uses metal electrodes attached to the monster's neck. This is probably not the best place to start. Your skin is a horrible conductor, so in order to bypass it, you are going to need about 600 volts—or enough to blow a hole in the skin. Those electrodes are also dangerously close to the **brain stem**. As the zombie chapter (p. 42) explains, your brain stem controls basic functions like breathing. Once your brain stem is fried by all that current, it can't tell your body to breathe. Breathing is kind of important to bring someone back to life. Better rethink that one, Doc.

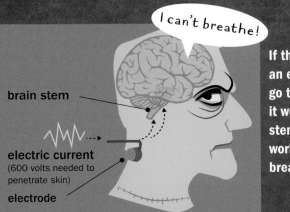

brain stem

electric current
(600 volts needed to
penetrate skin)

electrode

I can't breathe!

If the monster had an electric current go through his neck, it would fry his brain stem. Without a working brain stem, breathing would stop.

So the monster's brain is toast, but what about his heart? Today, we use a machine called a **defibrillator** that uses an electric current to shock a person's heart into working normally again after cardiac arrest. During cardiac arrest, a heart beats with an erratic, rapid rhythm that "arrests," or stops, the heart's ability to pump blood. A defibrillator does not restart a heart in the same way that a dead car battery might be recharged. Instead, a defibrillator works by disrupting the unnatural rhythm with an electrical shock so that the heart can return to a normal, steady beat.

Now, you might have seen the following scene in a medical TV drama: a sick patient is hooked up to an electrocardiogram (EKG) that bleeps, steadily measuring the electrical activity of the heart. Then, all of a sudden, the electrical spikes flatten to a straight line accompanied by one long *bleeeeeeeeeep*. The patient has flatlined. The doctors start running around frantically, grabbing paddles, and screaming "code something-or-another."

Yeah, that never happens in real life. Unfortunately, if an EKG indicates a flat line, no amount of electricity is going to get that heart beating again. A flat line means that there is zero electric current, and a defibrillator must have an electric current to work with. There are other drugs that can stimulate a heart to beat again, but if you were to repeatedly send more

electricity through a dead heart, you would only get a crispy, dead heart with a horrible burnt-flesh smell.

What is somewhat accurate in Frankenstein's monster-comes-to-life scene is all that twitching. Whenever an electric current is passed through a body, the muscles contract. (Remember Galvani's experiments on very dead frogs.) Electricity makes muscles spasm because our nervous system carries an electrical charge, and those nerves and muscle cells continue to conduct electricity whether there is life or not. In Frankenstein's case, the monster's body could be made to jerk just like Galvani's creepy, twitching frog legs. However, there's more to life than a few muscle twitches.

WHICH WOULD RESTART A FLATLINED HEART?

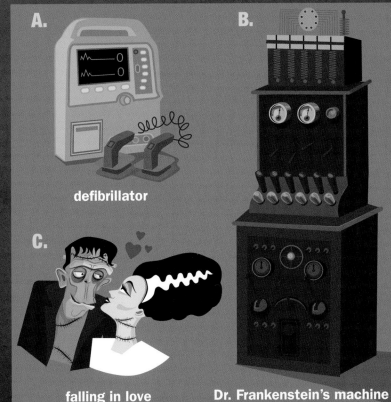

A.

defibrillator

B.

C.

falling in love

Dr. Frankenstein's machine

THE MONSTROUS HISTORY OF ELECTRICITY

2750 BCE
A FISHY CURE
The ancient Greeks use electric rays to numb headaches after observing the jolts coming out of them.

1752
FRANKLIN DOESN'T ELECTROCUTE HIMSELF
Benjamin Franklin hypothesizes that lightning and electricity are similar. To prove his hypothesis, he flies a kite in a thunderstorm with a metal key attached to it. The metal key draws electricity from the lightning and sparks jump from the key to his knuckle.

Scientists today have tried to replicate Franklin's experiment only to discover that it is a good way to electrocute yourself. For this reason, many historians doubt the details of the experiment.

Amber has a neutral charge until the friction from rubbing the cat causes it to pick up electrons and have a negative charge that attracts the cat's fur.

600 BCE
FRAIDY-CATS
Greek philosopher Thales of Miletus observes that amber rubbed on a cat's fur can attract small objects. This is an example of static electricity.

Franklin used electricity to electrocute turkeys for amused dinner guests.

1800
A JOLT OF KNOWLEDGE
Questioning Galvani's experiments, scientist Alessandro Volta uses stacks of two different metal discs with brine-soaked paper in between them. He then connects his apparatus to two probes, which he inserts into his ears. He manages not to electrocute himself and realizes the electric current is not coming from any animal electricity inside his head. Instead, the two differently charged metals with a conductor in between is what really creates an electric current. Volta's discovery of electric current leads to the voltaic pile, or first battery.

1800s
FIRST ELECTRICAL MACHINES

The first electrical machines use a hand crank to rub a glass wheel against two leather, hair-filled, pads coated with a conductor material, usually gold. As the wheel spins, the friction of the glass against the pads creates a positive charge, which is collected into brass cylinders.

People lined up to experience a jolt from these new electrical machines. Many reported nosebleeds and headaches afterward.

1899
SICK AS A DOG

Physiologists Frederic Batelli and Jean-Louis Prévost experiment with defibrillation on dogs. A defibrillator restores natural rhythms by delivering an electrical shock to the heart. Batelli and Prevost discover they could save the dogs with the correct amount of current (and kill them with the wrong amount).

1880s
THOMAS EDISON: GENIUS, INVENTOR . . . ANIMAL KILLER

Westinghouse Electric acquires inventor Nikola Tesla's patents for alternating current, or AC current—current that reverses direction. This launches a feud with the competing Edison Company, which supplies direct current, or DC current—current that runs in a single direction. In what became known as the War of the Currents, Thomas Edison tries to discredit his rival and show AC current is too dangerous for homes by staging public executions—frying dogs, cats, and horses. Despite the scare tactics, AC current becomes the preferred method to power homes.

1890
LITTLE MONSTERS

Thomas Edison uses his experiments with the first recorded sound on a line of talking dolls he calls his little monsters. The dolls mostly creep people out and were a complete flop.

The first motion pictures exhibited in the United States were by Edison's production company, Edison Studios. One of the first films made was *Frankenstein* in 1910.

THE MONSTER MASH-UP: FRANKENSTEIN SCIENCE & GENETICS

In the movie, Dr. Frankenstein cobbles together a man by stealing different body parts from graveyards. We may not be able to mix and match body parts yet, but an organism's traits can be changed in a laboratory. Instead of organisms inheriting genes from their parents, scientists now can artificially transfer the genes of one species into another species. This new science is called transgenesis, and it has become a hotly debated practice due to the ethical issues it raises. Many people fear the science will someday be used on humans to create Frankenstein-like monsters . . .

Please don't give me eight legs!

WHAT ARE GENES?
Your genes are the set of instructions you inherit from your parents that determine traits such as eye color, hair color, and your killer science skills.

The silk-weaving gene from spiders is combined with a goat's DNA.

The gene causes the goat to produce silk protein in its milk.

Silk is extracted from the milk and spun into thread.

SPIDER-SILK GOATS

Humans have a conflicted relationship with spiders. We are terrified of them but fascinated by the silk threads they weave into their webs. Because spider silk is stronger than steel but also lightweight and elastic, scientists have recognized its potential to make stronger bulletproof vests, safer car airbags, and more flexible sutures for surgery. Unfortunately, spiders cannot be farmed like silk worms because they have the inconvenient habit of eating one another when kept in close proximity. So pioneering scientists took the silk-making gene from spiders and put it into the milk-producing DNA in goats. These "spider-goats" look like normal goats, but they produce silk in their milk that scientists can then separate out. And unlike spiders, these part-goat/part-spider animals have no desire to eat one another . . . yet.

MIGHTY MOUSE

In a 2007 experiment on mice, scientists modified the gene that turns glucose, the simple sugars found in foods, into energy. The super mice with the modified gene ran an astonishing 3.7 miles (6 km) at a speed of 65 feet (20 m) per minute for five hours. These mice need to eat more, but they don't get muscle cramps, are half the weight of normal mice, and live three years longer. They also are more aggressive. Let's hope these mice are used to fight for good and not evil.

GLOW-IN-THE-DARK PIGS

Scientists created pigs that glow green under black light by injecting jellyfish DNA into pig embryos. (Thankfully, the pigs did not inherit the jellyfish's stinging abilities, and they are as healthy as regular pigs.) These glowing pigs are special because they are genetic markers. Genetic markers work just as they sound—they mark when a gene has been successfully incorporated into a species. Currently, this research is being used to study hemophilia—a rare genetic disease in which the gene that allows blood to clot is missing or defective. People who suffer from hemophilia can have excessive bleeding from even minor cuts, but these luminescent swine have given scientists hope that they may someday find a cure.

SPINACH PIGS

Most people would argue that bacon doesn't need to be messed with, but scientists just can't leave well enough alone. Spinach pigs were created by taking a gene from spinach plants and transferring them into fertilized pig eggs. By doing this, scientists made pigs that are leaner and therefore healthier to eat. While spinach pigs might not turn sausage into diet food, it does create meat with some of the health benefits of spinach. Scientists are predicting that livestock with plant genes, such as spinach pigs, will be in the grocery store within ten years. Until then, you could just try eating spinach.

THE BELTSVILLE PIG

The Beltsville pig is the classic tale of science gone horribly wrong. In hopes of creating pigs with less fat, Beltsville pigs were given the gene for human growth hormone—the hormone that promotes lean, strong muscles and helps delay aging. Unfortunately, these little piggies never quite made it to market. The pigs did have less body fat, but they also had a slew of health problems: painful joints, diabetes, diarrhea, heart disease, ulcers, a weakened immune system, bulging eyes, and thickened skin. Seventeen of the nineteen Beltsville pigs died before their first birthday.

REAL MONSTERS: TRUE TALES OF MAD DOCTORS

Dr. Frankenstein's experiments may seem bizarre, but the following mad scientists also pushed the ethical boundaries of science:

JOHN HARVEY KELLOGG
FRANKENSTEIN GETS A CEREAL

Scientists are always trying to come up with ways to control human behavior, and Dr. John Harvey Kellogg thought he had the answer—cornflakes. Or to be more precise, tasteless cornmeal baked into tooth-cracking, hard biscuits. Kellogg believed a bland diet was the secret to health, while rich food led to illness. Unfortunately, no one wanted to eat Kellogg's cornflakes until his brother added the secret ingredient: sugar. Years later, cereal manufacturers kept adding more and more sugar until they had a breakfast food that would send any monster into a diabetic coma. Other weird science followed. When Franken Berry cereal was first introduced in 1971, the cereal got its powder-pink color from Red Dye No. 2 and 3. It also had the nasty side effect of turning kids' poop pink because the dyes were indigestible. Many parents rushed their kids to the ER complaining of pink poop. The dye's formula has since been changed. Or so we hope . . .

When Franken Berry cereal was first introduced in 1971, it terrified parents. The dyes in it caused kids to poop pink.

SIDNEY GOTTLIEB
DR. FEELGOOD

Everyone knows drugs are bad for you, but in the 1960s, Sidney Gottlieb believed he could use the hallucinogenic drug lysergic acid diethylamide, otherwise known as LSD, to control minds. Gottlieb worked for the CIA on a top secret program called MK-Ultra in which he drugged human guinea pigs with LSD. The hope was that the CIA could use the drug to force enemies to reveal secrets. Gottlieb enlisted several artists and writers for his experiments, including author Ken Kesey. Kesey went on to write his famous novel, *One Flew over the Cuckoo's Nest,* about a rebellious mental patient subjected to mind-controlling drugs, shock therapy, and a lobotomy (see next page).

Author Ken Kesey took part in Gottlieb's CIA-run experiments with LSD. At the time, he did not realize the drug was harmful. LSD later became illegal in 1968.

WALTER FREEMAN
A PIECE OF YOUR MIND

In *Frankenstein*, the monster cannot control his impulsive behavior and kills his creator's wife. If he had lived in the 1960s, doctors might have treated the monster's aggression with a lobotomy—a brain surgery that severs the nerves in the front part of the brain called the prefrontal lobe. The lobotomy was developed by Dr. António Egas Moniz in 1936, but it was Walter Freeman who "perfected" it years later. In a typical lobotomy, Freeman hammered through the tear ducts in the eyeballs into the brain with an ice pick-shaped tool and then swirled it around as if he were mashing up an avocado. The lobotomy could be completed in under ten minutes, and Freeman often demonstrated its simplicity by performing it with his left hand (he was right-handed) and sometimes hammering through both eyes at once. The results were mixed. The lucky ones just became more docile. The unlucky ones became incapacitated or died. Freeman mashed up about four thousand brains before doctors realized the lobotomy was hurting patients.

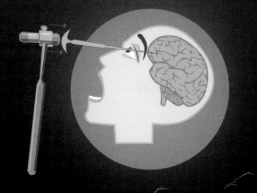

VLADIMIR DEMIKHOV
TWO HEADS ARE BETTER THAN ONE

In the movie *Frankenstein*, the mad scientist transplants a head onto a body to create his monster. Head transplants may seem like sci-fi horror, but it has been done. In 1954, Dr. Vladimir Demikhov created the first surgically-made two-headed dog. Demikhov performed the experiment several times, and his most successful pair of canines lived twenty-nine days. Are human head transplants in our future?

ROBERT J. WHITE
THE HEAD SWITCHEROO

In *Frankenstein*, no amount of whacks to the noggin could have tamed the monster, but perhaps a new head would have helped? In 1970, Dr. Robert J. White performed the first successful head transplant when he sewed a rhesus monkey head onto a different monkey body. Although the new monkey head could see and taste, it was paralyzed from the head down because the spinal column could not be attached. This alone should make human head transplants seem like a horrible idea, but such is never the case. Italian neurosurgeon Sergio Canavero has claimed he will perform the first human head transplant, but he has yet to do so. Many doctors don't believe it can be done and worry about the psychological impacts of such a switch.

Could you someday swap heads with someone? The hope is that head transplants will help people who are paralyzed. The fear is that it will create monsters.

DRACULA

You never want to anger authors, or they might put you in their next book as a bloodsucking vampire. The story of Dracula may be a fictional tale, but it was inspired by some very real people.

Remember those creative kids who were cooped up writing ghost stories in the "Frankenstein" chapter? Well, that must have been one heck of a writing retreat because not only did Mary Shelley (then Mary Godwin) begin to write *Frankenstein* at the get-together, but there was another author with a penchant for monster tales at the same party. He was Dr. John William Polidori, and he was the personal physician to Lord Byron. Unfortunately, the poet's and the doctor's egos clashed from the start. In his diary, Byron complained about his physician's "vanity and youth," and it wasn't long before Byron fired "poor Dr. Polidori."

Luckily, the good doctor found revenge-writing therapeutic. In 1816, he wrote, *The Vampyre, a Tale*, about a charming aristocrat capable of seducing innocent women while also draining their last drop of blood. He modeled his fictional vampire after Lord Byron and made sure everyone knew it.

Three years earlier, Lady Caroline Lamb had created a scandal by writing a tell-all novel about a bad boy named "Lord Ruthven," who was based on her ex-boyfriend—none other than Lord Byron. (Byron had his share of angry exes.) What did Dr. Polidori name his vampire? Lord Ruthven, of course.

After its release, *The Vampyre* became the talk of Europe. Several vampire tales followed (see timeline on p. 28), but the one that truly captured the public's imagination was *Dracula*, written by Irish novelist Bram Stoker in 1897. While it is obvious Dr. Polidori was grinding axes instead of wooden stakes, scholars are still quibbling about what inspired Stoker's vampire.

Stoker did leave research notes, and from those notes, we know he borrowed the name Dracula from a real-life prince of Wallachia (modern-day Romania) named Vlad Dracula, otherwise known as Vlad the Impaler. Good ole Vlad made shish kebab out of his enemies by running long stakes through them and then leaving them to the vultures. He was both feared and loved in his time. The name Drăculea (Dracula) was typically given to rulers who were valiant, cunning, and a bit cruel. We know Stoker was aware of this fact because he wrote in his notes, using caps, "DRACULA in Wallachian language means DEVIL." (It also can be translated as "Dragon.")

Both the fictional Dracula and the real Dracula resided in castles, but that's really where the similarities end. Stoker's Dracula was a count (Vlad was a prince) and lived in Transylvania (not Wallachia). Stoker's Dracula also drank blood (Vlad did a lot of heinous things, but drinking blood was not in his bag of tricks).

Another likely source of inspiration for Dracula was Stoker's enigmatic boss Henry Irving. Irving was one of the most famous actors of the British stage, and from the moment Stoker met him, he was "spellbound." Irving even resembled Stoker's physical description of Dracula down to his "massive eyebrows," "thin nose," "domed forehead, and hair growing scantily round the temples."

Stoker became Irving's stage manager, and much like personal assistants today, Stoker worked tirelessly for him, not only becoming Irving's lackey but also writing his speeches and

"My revenge has just begun! I spread it over centuries and time is on my side."
—**Dracula**

answering all Irving's letters (an estimated half million letters over his lifetime). Stoker became so sucked into the orb of his demanding boss that one wonders how he ever had time to write a novel. Stoker never complained (he wasn't the complaining type), but he may have taken out some workplace frustrations by putting pen to paper.

In return, Irving tolerated Stoker as long as he kept the spotlight where it belonged—on Irving. He was often dismissive of Stoker's talents and paid little attention to his employee's writing aspirations. When *Dracula* was performed at the Lyceum Theatre, Irving shook his head in disgust and summed up what he thought of it with one word: "Dreadful."

Sadly, Stoker died in poverty, and we still know very little about the man behind *Dracula*. When asked, he didn't like to talk about who inspired his blood-thirsty count and he would even sometimes teasingly claim that his vampire came to him in a nightmare after eating too much "dressed crab." (The crab became a family joke.)

KILLING A VAMPIRE . . . MEDIEVAL STYLE

When archaeologists discover a burial containing skeletons treated as if they were dangerous, they call them "**deviant burials**." Historians are still not sure if these graves contain suspected vampires or just criminals. What is certain is that the living feared the dead would escape.

The Vampire Grim Reaper
In 2009, in Drawsko, Poland, skeletons were found with iron sickles across the necks. In folklore, iron was believed to keep vampires down.

VAMPIRES FROM FOLKLORE: NOT A LOT OF SPARKLE

We tend to think of vampires like Dracula as beautiful, sparkly people, but the first vampires of European folklore weren't so pretty. Vampires from the fifteenth to the seventeenth centuries were not even called vampires. (That word was not used until the eighteenth century.) They were called **revenants**, and they arose from the grave looking bloated, messy, and hungry for blood (or flesh). Their sole purpose was to terrorize the living, and they often brought death and disease in their wake.

In 2004, archaeologists were searching for the site of a medieval bishop's palace in Kilteasheen, Ireland, when they came across a very different discovery—a burial site containing close to three thousand skeletons. On the outskirts of the burial site, archaeologists found two skeletons buried with baseball-sized rocks wedged into their mouths. Even more puzzling, forensic pathologists determined the rocks were placed in their mouths *after* their deaths. Were the rocks shoved in their mouths to prevent them from feeding on the living?

The skeletons were believed to be victims of the bubonic plague—an infectious disease that ravaged Europe killing half the population in some areas. So many people died that it became difficult to bury the dead. Often villagers just dug shallow graves and dumped the bodies on top of one another, layer after layer. Feral dogs pawed the earth looking for fresh corpses, dragging off decrepit arms, legs, and feet into nearby villages. Can you imagine seeing your neighbor's dog with a random, rotting leg in his mouth? These desperate times led to some very desperate measures to stop the spread of plague—and to contain the vampires.

Today we know diseases are spread by bacteria and viruses, usually from person to person, and not from the undead coming back to feast on the living. European medieval folk didn't have science to battle these monsters, so they turned to superstitions and left some very strange clues on how to keep suspected vampires in their graves.

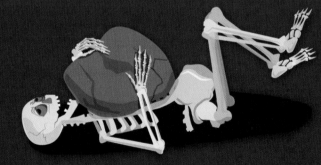

Wicked and Weighed Down
In the early 1990s in Čelákovice, Czech Republic, fourteen skeletons were found with large boulders placed across the chests. The victims are believed to have all died in the twelfth or thirteenth century, probably from a plague **epidemic**.

Cross My Heart . . . and Hope NOT to Die
In the early 1990s, three boys were playing on a hillside in Griswold, Connecticut, when two skulls rolled down the hill after them. A grave site was later discovered containing twenty-nine skeletons from the mid-nineteenth century. All the skeletons had a normal burial except one, a male skeleton with a decapitated head and leg bones arranged in the shape of a skull and crossbones. Researchers believe the bones were arranged to prevent him from escaping his grave.

The Vampire of Venice
In 2006, in Venice, Italy, a roughly sixty-one- to seventy-one-year-old female skeleton was found with a large rock in her mouth. Forensic pathologists were able to determine from the teeth that the rock was placed and not violently shoved into the skull, most likely after her death.

THE DEAD VS. THE UNDEAD

Before the early twentieth century, many vampire fears arose out of simply not understanding the science of death. How a body changes after death is called **decomposition**. The process begins with tiny microscopic living organisms called bacteria. Bacteria are on the surface of this book, inside your body, and in the food you eat. You also have bacteria inside your stomach. When you are alive, one of the many jobs of the gut bacteria (called intestinal flora) is to break down food and convert it into nutrients your body can use for fuel. When you die, the bacteria inside your digestive system still continue to work hard, but they no longer break down food. Instead, they break down your body . . . by slowly consuming your organs.

When these intestinal bacteria eat, they produce gas. A lot of gas. This means dead bodies bloat, not because they have gorged on a feast of blood, but for the same reason that living bodies bloat—because gases inside the stomach need an escape route. Some corpses will blow up two to three times their original size until, like a balloon, they deflate. Not only can they deflate, they can sometimes pop. (This can lead to a room-clearing fart that coroners claim smells a bit like flatulence and vomit combined.) When a body pops underground, the corpse will move and shift to a new position. Even more suspicious,

because gases in the body, such as methane, are lighter than air, bodies not buried deep enough will rise to the surface, making it seem as if they are up to no good. Can you imagine burying a dead person and later finding it in a different position near the surface? The dead are not supposed to move.

Driving a stake through the chest doesn't help matters. Think of what happens when a balloon suddenly lets out air. It kind of makes a shrieking noise, right? You can imagine how that must have freaked medieval people out. And that's not the only strange noise dead bodies can make. The dead also groan. When the abdominal wall bursts, it makes a noise that sounds like a pig snacking on garbage. Medieval people even had a name for it—*sonus porcinus*, Latin for "noisy swine."

These same gases that build up in the intestines can cause a red-brown fluid called **purge fluid** to push up through the lungs and out of the mouth. Purge fluid resembles blood and appears at the corners of the mouth, as if the corpse had just fed and forgot to use a napkin. Sometimes these purge fluids will even slowly eat away at the shroud covering the face. Medieval people had not discovered intestinal bacteria yet, so to them, it just looked like grandma was feasting on blood after she had died.

The dead's teeth and nails can sometimes seem as if they are growing. After death, the flesh starts to shrivel up and is pulled back along the nail bed and gumline. This forces teeth and nails to become more prominent, making it *seem* as if they are longer. Ancient Egyptian embalmers were accustomed to dealing with dead people, so they put metal thimbles on fingers and toes to prevent the skin from shrinking. Medieval folk didn't use these tools because they didn't understand what was happening.

Decomposing bodies can also seem as if they have new skin. Pathologists call this phenomenon **skin slippage**. It occurs when the top layers of skin separate from the body, revealing the white-and-pink layer underneath. All this activity can even cause the corpse's temperature to increase, as if they are not cold and lifeless but living.

Now that you know how decomposition works, you might be thinking, "Sheeesh, those medieval people were pretty daft not to be able to tell the difference between dead people and vampires." But the science behind death is not always straightforward. There are many factors that can affect decomposition, including temperature, humidity, insects, or even the placement of the body. The shape of the body when alive will also affect how rapidly it decomposes—including weight, gender, and age. Even what you were doing when you died can alter decomposition. For example, if you were taking down a zombie hoard before your death, you will decompose faster due to more lactic acid in your muscles. With death so unpredictable, it is easy to see why people relied on superstition over science.

UNDEAD OR DEAD?
HOW TO TELL THE DIFFERENCE

UNDEAD
They have fangs for biting victims.
DEAD
The skin dehydrates and is pulled back along the gumline, making teeth more prominent.

UNDEAD
The body moves in the grave.
DEAD
A buildup of gases causes the body to shift positions.

UNDEAD
The stomach bloats after feeding.
DEAD
Gases build up in the stomach, causing bloating.

UNDEAD
New skin forms because the monster is regenerating.
DEAD
Skin slippage causes the body to appear as if it is regenerating.

UNDEAD
The body feels warm because it is not truly dead.
DEAD
Active bacteria cause the body to heat up.

UNDEAD
Hair keeps growing.
DEAD
The skin on the scalp shrinks and exposes more hair.

UNDEAD
Blood around the lips indicates the vampire has fed.
DEAD
Gases cause purge fluid to push up into the mouth.

UNDEAD
Claw marks are on the body from trying to escape the coffin.
DEAD
Maggots cause lacerations on the skin that look like claw marks.

UNDEAD
Smelly farts occur from consuming too much blood.
DEAD
Gas builds up in the body until it finds an escape route.

WARNING
Both the dead and undead may make a screaming sound if you drive a stake through the heart.

DRACULA'S BLOODLINE

C. 600 BCE
LILITU
ANCIENT BABYLONIA
Lilitu, or Lilith, is believed to be a demon that feeds on the blood of babies. To protect their children, parents hang amulets around the baby's cradle.

C. 500 BCE
VETALA
ANCIENT INDIA
According to superstition, Vetala hangs upside down outside cemeteries and waits to feed on the blood of the dead.

C. 400 BCE
THE LAMIA
ANCIENT GREECE
The beautiful queen of Libya was turned into a child-devouring monster with a serpent tail. She has the ability to remove her eyes and feeds on the blood of young men.

1196
WILLIAM OF NEWBURGH'S CHRONICLES
English chronicler William of Newburgh first publishes stories of revenants that are believed to rise from the grave and suck the blood of the living.

1431–1477
PRINCE VLAD DRĂCULEA
Vlad Dracula of Wallachia impales his enemies upon sharp stakes and earns the name Vlad the Impaler. Bram Stoker later borrows his name for the main character in his vampire novel, *Dracula*.

1486
MALLEUS MALEFICARUM
Used mainly as a witch-hunters' guide by the Catholic Church, *Malleus Maleficarum* (*Hammer of Witches*) also spreads fear of vampires by claiming the devil used corpses to rise and attack the living.

15TH–16TH CENTURIES
THE VAMPIRE PLAGUES
In central Europe, belief in vampires becomes widespread, especially in rural villages. Vampires are blamed for causing the bubonic plague and kept in their graves with rocks, stakes, and iron chains.

1610
COUNTESS ELIZABETH BÁTHORY
Elizabeth Báthory tortures and murders young servant girls in her Hungarian castle. She is rumored to bathe in their blood in an attempt to stay young.

A HISTORY OF BLOODLUST

1730s
PANIC SPREADS . . .
The vampire epidemic hits Europe, and scholars begin publishing articles on vampire behavior.

1732
VISUM ET REPERTUM (SEEN AND DISCOVERED)
Austrian field surgeon Johann Flückinger performs autopsies on the corpses of suspected "vampirs" who refuse to decompose in their grave, and he publishes his observations. It becomes a best seller and establishes much of what we know of vampires today.

1755
NOT EVERYONE WAS A BELIEVER
After a suspected female vampire is dug up and beheaded, Empress Maria Theresa forbids vampire hunting.

"Nothing was spoken of but vampires, from 1730–1735."
—Voltaire, eighteenth-century philosopher

1819
THE VAMPYRE, A TALE BY DR. JOHN POLIDORI
Polidori publishes his scandalous novel about a bloodsucking demon based on heartthrob Lord Byron. For the first time, vampires are attractive and seen as romantic.

1872
CARMILLA
Joseph Sheridan Le Fanu writes one of the first popular vampire novels about a vampire named Carmilla who drinks blood, walks through walls, and turns into a cat.

"You must come with me, loving me, to death; or else hate me, and still come with me."
—J. Sheridan Le Fanu, *Carmilla*

1897
DRACULA
While working as Henry Irving's assistant, Bram Stoker writes *Dracula*, about a Transylvanian vampire that bears an uncanny resemblance to his boss. Most of the proceeds from his book went to Stoker's publisher, and he died in poverty.

"Persons of small courage and weak nerves should confine their reading of these gruesome pages strictly to the hours between dawn and sunset."
—*Daily Mail* (London), 1897

1922
NOSFERATU
The first adaptation of *Dracula* hits the silver screen. The main character is Count Orlok, and the film follows the same plot as Stoker's *Dracula*. Stoker's wife sues for copyright infringement and wins. She demands all copies of the movie be destroyed, but some survive.

1931
DRACULA, UNIVERSAL STUDIOS
Universal Studio's version stars Bela Lugosi as Dracula. Lugosi later turns down another monster hit, *Frankenstein* (1931).

IT'S REALLY "BLOODCURDLING"
Research shows watching scary movies increases levels of a certain clotting protein in our bloodstreams.

1958
HORROR OF DRACULA
This Technicolor film stars Christopher Lee as Dracula and is based on Bram Stoker's novel.

1972
COUNT VON COUNT
Sesame Street's favorite counting count teaches kids math. The count is based on the vampire folklore beliefs that vampires have arithmomania—a compulsion to count.

1987
THE LOST BOYS
A cast of heartthrobs teams up for this punk rock 80s drama set in a fictional California town. The main character, Michael, broods until he reluctantly gives into his base vampire desires, which inevitably leads to the ultimate battle of good vs. evil.

1994
INTERVIEW WITH THE VAMPIRE
Based on the best-selling novel by Anne Rice, the Vampire Chronicles series stars Tom Cruise as Lestat de Lioncourt—an eighteenth-century French nobleman turned into a vampire—and Brad Pitt as his conflicted vampire sidekick.

1992
FRANCIS FORD COPPOLA'S DRACULA
Another remake of Bram Stoker's *Dracula*—except this *Dracula* begins with the tale of Vlad the Impaler, who awakens in Victorian London and sets out to avenge the death of his wife.

UNHAPPY VAMPIRES
Brad Pitt hated playing the role of vampire Louis de Pointe du Lac so much that he asked the producer how much it would cost to get out of the role. With a price tag of $40 million, Pitt decided to stick it out.

1997
BUFFY THE VAMPIRE SLAYER
Popular TV show *Buffy the Vampire Slayer*, based loosely on the 1992 film, stars Sarah Michelle Gellar as the Chosen One—a vampire slayer with some kick-butt moves and a hoard of high school buddies to fight the forces of darkness.

BUFFY
More papers, essays, and books have been devoted to *Buffy the Vampire Slayer* than any other TV show.

2008
TWILIGHT SAGA
Based on Stephenie Meyer's vampire romance saga, Bella Swan (Kristen Stewart) falls in love with one-hundred-year-old vampire Edward Cullen (Robert Pattinson). Edward warns Bella that he can tear her apart any minute, and so begins the comeback of the teen vampire thriller.

WHERE SHOULD A VAMPIRE BITE?

Vampires can choose from two delicious types of blood-filled vessels—arteries or veins. Veins (1) are blood vessels that carry blood back to the heart. Arteries (2) are blood vessels that carry oxygenated blood away from the heart.

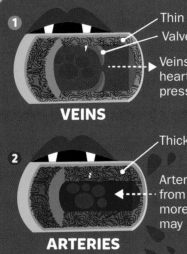

Thin walls are easy to pierce.
Valves regulate blood flow.

Veins pump blood to the heart, so there is less pressure and more blood.

VEINS

Thick walls are hard to pierce.

Arteries pump blood away from the heart, so there is more pressure. Arteries may spurt when punctured.

ARTERIES

IF YOU ARE A NICE VAMPIRE

There are several reasons why a vein is a better choice for bloodlust than an artery. Veins are closer to the skin's surface and easier for fangs to pierce. Veins also have thinner walls, so the vampire does not need to bite down with as much force. They also can hold more blood, so the vampire doesn't need to suck as hard.

He seemed nice until he bit my carotid artery.

CAROTID ARTERY
A lack of oxygenated blood to the brain will cause quick death.

JUGULAR VEIN
This spot is easy to access. It is closer to the skin's surface.

ASCENDING AORTA

DESCENDING AORTA
Fangs cannot reach these easily. The thick walls are hard to puncture.

MEDIAN CUBITAL VEIN
Doctors prefer this vein for drawing blood. It is a good choice for kind vampires.

BASILIC VEIN
It provides low pressure with a steady flow and is a great choice for nice vampires.

FEMORAL ARTERY
High pressure can cause spurting and a messy meal.

FEMORAL VEIN
It is not easy to get at. The victim can kick the vampire.

A healthy person can lose 10 to 15 percent of total blood volume before starting to suffer ill effects.

IF YOU ARE A MONSTROUS VAMPIRE

If you are a vampire and want to drain your victim to the last drop of blood quickly, then you might want to choose the carotid artery in the neck. The carotid artery carries oxygenated blood to the brain. If you suck from there, the person will start to get dizzy and not put up much of a fight.

Unfortunately, biting a major artery is messy. Because arteries contain more blood and are pumping blood away from the heart, they have far more pressure. More pressure means when you puncture them, they spurt. This would be like stabbing a hole in a running garden hose and then trying to drink from the hole. Arteries are also thicker and more elastic, so puncturing them is going to take a greater bite force. Understandably, vampires might not want to go through this extra work.

Lastly, it is really rude to bite someone's arteries. Arteries are deeper under the skin and have thicker walls, so it is going to hurt much more than biting a thinner-walled vein. For this reason, doctors typically draw blood from veins and not arteries.

IF YOU JUST WANT A SNACK

A vampire would not need to be too exact on hitting an artery or a vein. Vampires could also feed more like vampire bats that simply bite into the skin, penetrate the outer layer, and then lap up the blood from the wound with their tongues. Since blood naturally clots, the vampire bat's saliva contains a special anticoagulant to keep the blood flowing. (Read more about vampire bats on p. 40.)

WHY VAMPIRES PREFER RED

The blood in your veins is dark red or maroon, while blood from your arteries is bright red. Although your veins appear blue from the outside, neither your blood nor your veins are ever blue unless you are a Smurf or an octopus. Veins look blue as a result of an optical illusion. Unlike arteries, they carry deoxygenated blood, which absorbs red light. Due to the lack of oxygen, when light hits the surface of your skin, most of the red light is absorbed, leaving blue light reflected back to your eye.

> Fruity notes with a deep red color. Must be from a vein.

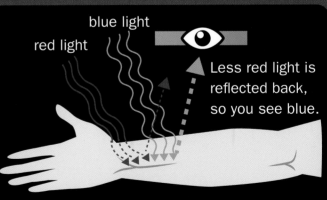

blue light

red light

Less red light is reflected back, so you see blue.

Veins carry deoxygenated blood, which absorbs more red light.

*Arteries are too deep under the skin to be seen from the surface.

33

HOW TO GET BLOOD THE RIGHT WAY

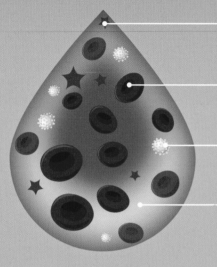

platelets
(less than 1%)
helps blood clot

red blood cells
(40–45%)
transports oxygen

white blood cells
(about 1%)
helps fight infection

plasma
(about 55%)
transports nutrients,
hormones, and proteins

WHAT IS BLOOD?

Blood is the red, sticky, metallic-tasting liquid that circulates in your arteries, veins, and capillaries. Its main function is to transport oxygen, nutrients, waste products, and hormones throughout the body. Blood contains four components: red blood cells, white blood cells, plasma, and platelets.

PLEASE DON'T DRINK BLOOD

In movies, vampires allow humans to drink their blood to restore health. This is not recommended. Blood is toxic to humans because it contains too much iron. Iron is an essential mineral needed to transport oxygen, but when we ingest it, the body cannot excrete the excess and a dangerous overdose can occur. Aside from an iron overdose, drinking blood can also infect someone with dangerous blood-borne illnesses such as hepatitis B, hepatitis C, and HIV.

Don't drink blood unless you are a bat.

Vampire bats are able to drink blood because the microscopic organisms within the gut, called the **microbiome**, allow them to digest blood without triggering an immune response.

KNOW YOUR TYPE

In *Dracula*, Lucy Westenra wastes away from Count Dracula draining her blood every night. In a gallant effort to save her, four men give blood and a rudimentary blood transfusion is done. In real life, this would have most likely killed the poor girl.

If you have been attacked by a vampire (or have lost blood for other reasons), you may need a blood transfusion to reverse blood loss. Before performing a blood transfusion, doctors must match your blood type. You have a unique blood type inherited from your parents. Each blood type is distinguished by its antigens—tiny markers that

> Guess which blood type is the most delicious...

coat the surface of red blood cells. These markers classify blood types as A, B, AB, or O and are further divided into distinct varieties. For example, A blood types have A antigens. B types have B antigens. AB have both. And O has neither.

When someone gets a blood transfusion, the person's antigens must match the donated blood (see below). Mismatched blood types lead your antibodies to detect foreign antigens on the donated blood cells and attack them. This triggers an immune response of fever, chills, pain at the injection site and, if not reversed in time, organ failure and eventually . . . death. While most hospitals can match common blood types quickly, if you have a rare blood type, you may need to store it for emergency situations . . . like when vampires attack.

BLOOD TRANSFUSIONS

The first blood transfusions were done in the late 1660s, and they didn't go so well. Blood types had not been discovered yet, so sometimes people died—and sometimes they did not—and no one knew why. Often blood transfusions were done between animals and people. (This also didn't go so well.) In 1901, Karl Landsteiner was the first to discover blood typing, which would save millions of lives.

YOUR BLOOD TYPE

AB NEGATIVE, B NEGATIVE
Your blood type is extremely rare. You should probably avoid hungry vampires.

AB POSITIVE
You people just take, take, take (at least when it comes to blood). ABs can receive blood from anyone. The bad news is that people with AB blood are 82 percent more likely to suffer from dementia than those with O blood.

A NEGATIVE
You can only receive blood from A- or O- donors. You should be nice to those people.

O NEGATIVE
You can give blood to anyone. Everyone wants to be your friend.

B POSITIVE
Many brilliant authors have this blood type.*

A POSITIVE
If you get malaria, you have a higher chance of dying. You should avoid getting malaria.

O POSITIVE
O+'s have the most common blood type and are also at a lower risk for heart disease and inflammation. They also get bitten more by mosquitoes (and possibly vampires).

*I do not have the scientific data to back this up yet.

MOST COMMON BLOOD TYPES

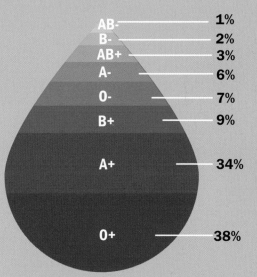

AB- — 1%
B- — 2%
AB+ — 3%
A- — 6%
O- — 7%
B+ — 9%
A+ — 34%
O+ — 38%

WHY BLOOD IS PRECIOUS
Scientists have yet to figure out how to make blood. The only way to get blood is from donors.

6.4 min. **15%**

Normal heart rate and blood pressure

 **8 min.** **15–<30%**

Rapid heart rate, sweating, dizziness, headache, and nausea may occur.

 10 min. **30–40%**

Rapid heart rate and decreased blood pressure. Pale, clammy skin along with blue lips and fingertips may occur.

 17 min. **>40%**

Rapid heart rate and decreased blood pressure continues. Loss of consciousness followed by death.

 **42.7 min.** **100%**

Dead

HEART RATE

Your heart rate, or pulse, is the number of times your heart beats per minute, or BPM.

BLOOD PRESSURE (BP)

Blood pressure is the strength of the blood against the artery walls. As blood volume drops, this pressure decreases. A low BP is dangerous because it decreases the blood supply to the brain.

TIP 2: STOP THE BLEEDING

Shallow puncture wounds from vampire fangs usually do not cause excessive bleeding unless you have encountered a vampire who went for the carotid artery (p. 32). If bleeding persists, apply gentle pressure with a bandage or soft cloth. Elevate the wound above the heart (if possible). If blood is spurting or bleeding does not stop, call 911 because the vampire has most likely bitten an artery. (Remember: Arteries will spurt and the blood will be bright red.)

TIP 3: CLEAN THE WOUND TO PREVENT INFECTION

A vampire, your dog, and your mom. They all share one thing in common: their mouths are really dirty. Roughly seven hundred types of bacteria live in the human mouth. Some of these bacteria are good—they help digest your food. And some are bad—they cause tooth decay and can spread infection. When you are alive, the good and bad bacteria live in a delicate balance. When you die, all bets are off. In all nonliving creatures, bacteria in the mouth feed on and decompose the body. (Reminder: Vampires are dead.)

SURVIVING VAMPIRES IN THE FUTURE . . .

In 2015 research began on EE-3-SO4—a drug that will save soldiers who suffer severe blood loss. EE-3-SO4 works not by halting bleeding but, instead, by helping the body respond better to severe blood loss and, therefore, giving the wounded more time to seek medical atttention. It counteracts the stages of blood loss by making the heart beat more efficiently, raising blood pressure, and pulling fluid from surrounding tissue to increase blood volume. The hope is that such drugs will not only save victims of vampire attacks, but also those who have lost blood from traumatic injuries.

Kiss me... My mouth is full of bacteria.

37

HOW TO BECOME AS IMMORTAL AS A VAMPIRE

In books and movies, vampires never age, but can someone truly live forever? Aging begins in the trillions of tiny building blocks called cells. Those cells make up your tissues, and those tissues make up organs like your eyes, skin, and heart. Inside each of these cells are threadlike structures called chromosomes. Chromosomes contain tightly packed molecules called DNA. Your DNA is arranged in different combinations to make up your genes—the set of instructions for all living things.

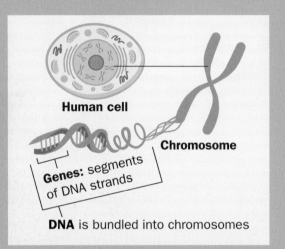

Human cell

Chromosome

Genes: segments of DNA strands

DNA is bundled into chromosomes

As you age, some of your cells divide and make new cells to replace the worn-out ones. When your cells divide, they make a copy of their DNA. During this process, the copy has to be an exact copy or mutations can occur, such as those that cause cancer.

Fortunately, your chromosomes have a way to protect your cells from making mistakes during cell division. At the end of your chromosomes are little caps called **telomeres**. These telomeres keep the DNA from becoming damaged. Think of telomeres as the eraser stub on the end of a pencil. They have the ability to prevent mistakes during cell division but, much like a pencil eraser, the more they get used, the more they get chewed up. Eventually, you are just left with a little stub and the metal scraping against paper.

That's when your cells say, "OK, I am tired. The jig is up. I am no longer going to divide if I can't stop mistakes."

When cells no longer divide, that is called **senescence**—a fancy word for aging. Senescence leads to disease, infection, wrinkles, and grandpa's (or grandma's) hair sprouting out of their nose. Scientists have estimated the amount of time a cell can divide throughout a human life to be roughly fifty-two times. This means that we actually have a biological clock ticking inside our bodies or that, like a fine cheese, we have an expiration date. In other words, we are all programmed to die.

Sure, it's a depressing thought. Death is inevitable. But before you decide to become a vampire so you will never get nose hairs, there is some good news. You also have immortal cells that never stop dividing. These cells have an enzyme called **telomerase** that restores telomeres back to their original shape. Cells that have telomerase include fetal cells, germ cells, and tumor cells that cause cancer. Unfortunately, this does not include normal human cells.

So how would a vampire keep its baby soft skin for thousands of years? One possibility is if its normal human cells accepted telomerase. Forcing these cells to accept telomerase has been done. In one recent experiment, researchers took the senescent cells (the ones that had stopped dividing) and fed telomerase into them. That's when something amazing happened—the cells started dividing again, thereby reversing the aging process. Although this has only been done on a small scale, the findings could mean we may someday be as immortal as vampires.

Until that day comes, there is something you can do to keep your telomeres as long as the day you were born. People who exercise regularly have longer telomeres. So go outside and pretend a hungry vampire is chasing you. If it catches you, tell the vampire you would rather wait for science to make you immortal.

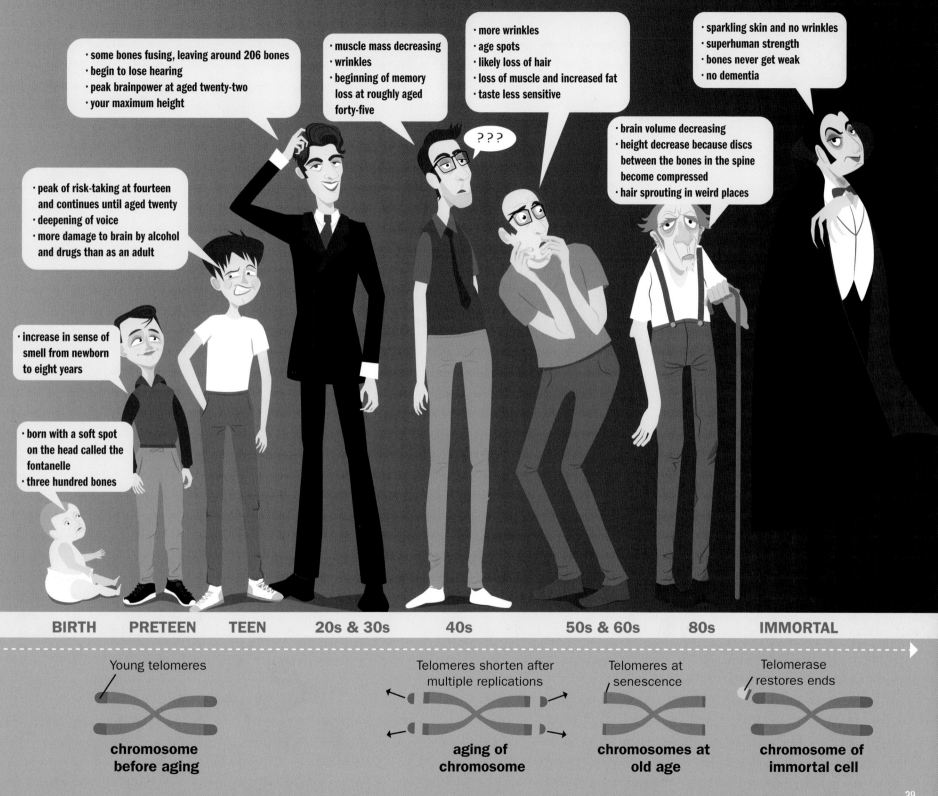

REAL MONSTERS: BLOODSUCKERS

Vampire bats are mostly found in Central and South America.

VAMPIRE MOTHS

We usually think of moths as those annoying fluttering things that put holes in our favorite sweater, but that was before scientists observed the vampire moth. Vampire moths feed by injecting their proboscis into their host and using it like a long straw to suck up blood. They then feed for up to fifty minutes and leave a red welt behind as their calling card.

Vampire finches do not attack humans . . . yet.

VAMPIRE BATS

You can run, but you can't hide from a vampire bat. They have special hearing to detect breathing, a keen sense of smell and sight, and wrinkly faces to feel the infrared heat coming off a warm body. Once they find their meal, vampire bats puncture the skin with tiny, sharp fangs and then release anticoagulants into the wound, which keep the blood flowing like a melting Slurpee. (The anticoagulant is appropriately named draculin.) But it is not their bloodlust that makes them monstrous. Vampire bats cause a type of rabies called "dumb rabies," which paralyzes its victims instead of turning them into raging lunatics. Fortunately, these bats prefer the blood of livestock.

Help! They ate my sweater and drank my blood.

VAMPIRE FINCHES

Call a bird a "booby," and it is bound to get picked on. Such is the case with the booby seabird, which is terrorized by the vampire finch of the Galápagos Islands. The vampire finch may look as cute as a button until you watch it peck, peck, peck at the booby with its sharp beak. Then as soon as enough pecking draws blood, his pals swarm in and have a feast.

They are cute until they drink your blood.

LEECHES

In *Dracula*, Jonathan Harker compares Count Dracula to "a filthy leech." Today, when we call someone a "leech," we mean they are being a mooch. The poor leech. We have been really unfair to this worm, considering no other bloodsucker has helped humans more. Throughout history, leeches were used to heal everything from headaches to fevers. In old English, *leech* meant "to heal," and medieval medical textbooks were called "leech books." Perhaps leeches are reviled because they don't have a

a leech bite

face, so it is hard to tell what they are feeling. Their suckers are on both ends, so we never know how to pick them up. They are hermaphrodites—they have both female and male sex organs. They avoid sunlight, a trait usually associated with vampires. And weirdest of all, when they bite, they leave behind an upside-down *Y* mark inside a circle, which looks suspiciously like a Mercedes logo.

Only the female mosquitoes bite.

MOSQUITOES

They are more than just buzzing pests. Mosquitoes cause more deaths than any other creature in the world—one million a year worldwide. Aside from spreading malaria and Zika virus and making that tropical rain forest vacation impossible, this bloodsucker may be in an evolutionary battle with us where either they or humans have to go. While only two hundred of the three thousand species of mosquitoes carry diseases, scientists have debated eradicating the bad ones by making the males sterile so no more baby mosquitoes can be born. Genetically modifying the biting females so they cannot host parasites has also been proposed. Either way, let this be a warning, mosquito!

Doctors today sometimes use leeches to help when reattaching limbs because the leech's saliva prevents blood from clotting.

Maybe I should have only eaten one...

LAMPREYS

This vampire fish mostly goes after other fish, sucking them dry, but they also have been known to attack humans. They have been especially problematic in the rivers of the UK, where they latch onto unsuspecting swimmers with their powerful suckers. Once one attaches, it can feed for days or weeks. Despite their mouths looking like suction cups with teeth, throughout history these fish have somehow been appetizing to humans. King Henry I of England supposedly died from gorging on a "surfeit of lampreys," and that was probably just one lamprey too many.

Why did you draw me with a face?

41

ZOMBIES

The first zombies were not the classic walking dead, flesh-eating variety but humans who were raised from the dead and put under mind control. Zombie stories originated in the seventeenth century in Haiti and were part of a collection of spirit-based beliefs known as vodou (or voodoo). The word *zombie* originated from the word *nzambi*, which is the name of the Bakongo people's supreme god.

It is said that a black magic priest, or bocor, turns a person into a zombie by giving them a potion to drink with enough bizarre ingredients to scare off Macbeth's witches. There are human bones, ground-up toad, and a hallucinogenic plant called the "zombie cucumber." But the real zinger in this zombie cocktail is tetrodotoxin, or "resurrection powder." Tetrodotoxin is a chemical found in the puffer fish that causes anyone who ingests it or even touches it to go into a deathlike state in which the heart slows and the person appears dead. The person will often have a blank stare and shallow breathing but can still manage simple, repetitive tasks like a mindless . . . well, zombie.

In 1929 travel writer William Seabrook researched rumors of such a zombie workforce in Haiti controlled by an organization called culte des morts (Cult of the Dead). According to Haitian folklore, the cult turned the dead into mindless zombies to work Haiti's sugarcane plantations. Seabrook's visit became the basis for his book *The Magic Island*, which became the inspiration for the first full-length zombie horror film—*White Zombie* (1932).

As you read this book, different parts of your brain are hard at work. Your **brain stem (A)** moves your eyes back and forth while billions of nerve cells, called neurons, light up like a computer switchboard. Don't worry if you don't remember those fancy names right now. Your horseshoe-shaped **hippocampus (B)** has committed these facts to memory.

How your brain works is a very complex process, which is why the 3 pounds (1.4 kg) of gray matter is a huge energy consumer. Even when you are not moving, your brain uses 20 percent of your total energy—more energy than any other organ in your body. So much energy that you're now hungry . . . at least your **hypothalamus (C)** is telling you so. You head to the fridge to make a salami sandwich. As the saltiness hits your tongue, your **thalamus (D)** relays sensory information like taste and smell. The snack has also made you tired. Your hypothalamus regulates

> I can't help it. My hypothalamus no longer works.

sleep patterns too, and it is starting to shut down and send signals that you need a nap. As you start to dream of unicorns or rainbows or showing up to school without clothes on, your entire brain becomes active.

Now imagine while you were sleeping, a zombie crept up behind you and chomped on your flesh. You are now dead. Sort of. Well, you're actually a zombie. Sorry about that.

But don't worry. Sure, your eyeball is dangling out of its socket, but it really isn't as bad as it looks. Parts of your brain still work. Unfortunately, while you were dead, the lack of oxygen destroyed other parts of your brain. Your **cerebellum (E)** has disintegrated to the point where you can only manage a lumbering gait and a blank stare. You try to call for help but can only groan because the area of your brain that controls language, called the **Broca's area (F)**, has turned to goo.

Things are getting worse. Your **hypothalamus (C)**, which was so great at regulating hunger earlier, is now on the fritz. Suddenly, that salami sandwich you ate for lunch doesn't seem to satisfy your hunger. You want more. Ten salami sandwiches or . . . some brains with a little pickle relish sounds scrumptious. No. No. You can't eat brains. That's disgusting, right? Well, it would be if your damaged **prefrontal cortex (G)** could still determine right from wrong. But it cannot.

You hit the fridge. The set of neurons no bigger than a fingernail located deep in the middle on either side of your brain, called the **amygdala (H)**, usually keeps your anger in check. Not this time. Your half-eaten amygdala has short-circuited, and you can no longer control your rage.

You look down at your hand. It is bleeding from hitting the fridge. The pain signals travel up your **brain stem (A)**, into your **thalamus (D)**, but you don't feel a thing because most of your thalamus was eaten by the zombie. Thanks a lot, zombie.

As your flesh begins to further decompose, your **basal ganglia (I)**, which are responsible for simple movements, allow you to shuffle to the door. But your hand can't turn the doorknob. (Remember, your **cerebellum (E)**, which controls fine motor skills, is toast.) So you smash the window open and shimmy through the hole.

"What is that delicious smell?" your **olfactory bulb (J)** asks. Just then, your postal carrier is at the door with a smile and the day's mail. You, of course, don't recognize him because your network of brain regions responsible for recognizing family and friends, called the **fusiform face area (K)**, no longer works. But your jaw sure does work (thanks to your basal ganglia). You bite down on the postal carrier's head. Mmmm . . . braaaaiiiiins.

THE ZOMBIE BRAIN

C: HYPOTHALAMUS
thirst, hunger, sleep, mood

G: PREFRONTAL CORTEX
impulse control, personality

D: THALAMUS
taste, smell, touch

I: BASAL GANGLIA
unthinking movements

K: FUSIFORM FACE AREA
recognizing faces

H: AMYGDALA
responding to fear

B: HIPPOCAMPUS
long-term memory

J: OLFACTORY BULB
detecting odors

F: BROCA'S AREA
speech and language
comprehension

E: CEREBELLUM
coordinating movements,
balance, speech

A: BRAIN STEM
breathing, swallowing, heart rate

■ NAMES OF PARTS OF THE BRAIN THAT NO LONGER WORK

■ NAMES OF PARTS OF THE BRAIN THAT STILL WORK

THE ZOMBIE VIRUS: WHY IT IS SCARY

I am way scarier than zombies...

CAN'T KEEP A DEAD PERSON DOWN

One of the reasons many plagues like the bubonic plague died out is because after they killed a portion of the population, there weren't enough people left to infect and keep the plague going. Although corpses do spread diseases, after proper burial (as in the dead not moving around), they don't cause any mischief. Most viruses need live, not dead, people to spread. Such is not the case with zombies. The dead can still spread the disease, and once they become zombies, there is no cure.

HUMANS ARE ALWAYS MESSING WITH SCIENCE

What if the rabies virus, which causes rage, combined with the West Nile virus, which causes memory loss, and then further combined with the measles virus, which is the most contagious virus? It would be a pretty dangerous virus and would make for another Hollywood drama. Luckily, viruses can't reshuffle like a deck of cards. For example, strains of the influenza virus (the flu) have mutated, but they were different variants of the same virus. If you combined different viruses, you would end up with a very dead virus instead of a deadlier virus.

One possible danger is if a virus was genetically engineered. A genetically engineered virus is one whose genes have been modified. Using today's technology, a virus's genetic material can be inserted into host cells, but scientists have yet to combine two viruses to get a new virus. Until that changes, your best bet is to be prepared for the zombie apocalypse (see p. 52).

DIFFICULT TO CONTAIN

Another advantage a zombie virus would have is that containing infected individuals would be difficult. For example, if you got the flu, you would skip school and stay in bed. You certainly don't want to get anyone sick. But if you got a zombie virus, you would prefer to eat your teacher instead of staying in bed sipping chicken soup. Sick people who were motivated to move around would definitely make a virus spread faster.

REAL MONSTERS: THE GREAT INFLUENZA OF 1918

Calls of "Bring out your dead!" could be heard from inside the houses of the living. To keep up with the removal of bodies, highway workers dug large trenches and dumped the corpses one on top of another, like layers of a lasagna. The plague was so virulent that some survivors reported their loved ones were fine one minute and then turning blue a few hours later, their lungs drowning in their own mucus. This isn't some hellscape scene out of a zombie apocalypse movie but real-life eyewitness testimonials recorded in 1918. The "plague" was the great influenza, or Spanish flu, and in the United States it killed 675,000 people in less than three months. That's more than the number of people from the US who died in all the wars of the twentieth century combined. And unlike today's flu, which usually only kills the elderly and very sick, the 1918 influenza attacked people in the prime of their life. Those between the ages of twenty-five and twenty-nine had the highest death rates, and we still don't know why.

STATES WHERE YOU ARE MOST LIKELY TO BE
EATEN BY A ZOMBIE

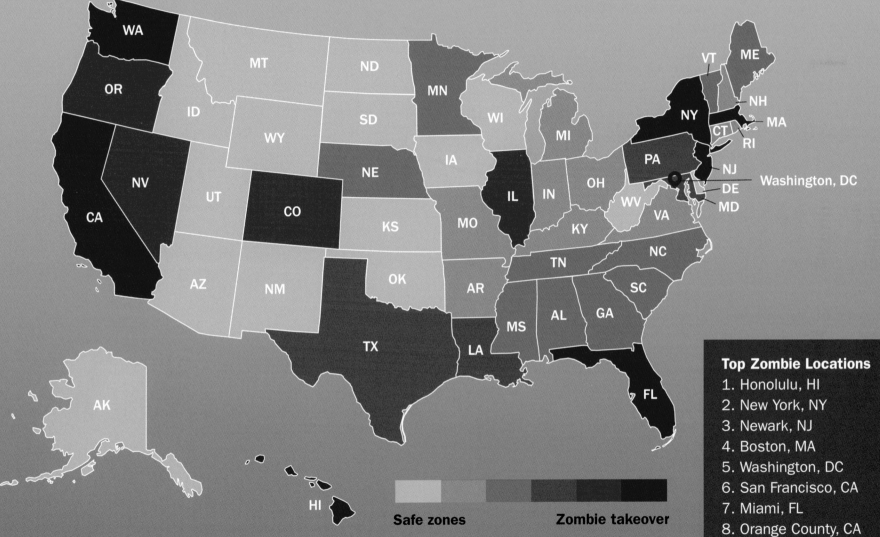

Safe zones   Zombie takeover

Top Zombie Locations
1. Honolulu, HI
2. New York, NY
3. Newark, NJ
4. Boston, MA
5. Washington, DC
6. San Francisco, CA
7. Miami, FL
8. Orange County, CA
9. Los Angeles, CA
10. Seattle, WA

To determine the most dangerous states, the following criteria were used:

1. Population data. The most congested areas will result in the most zombies.

2. A walking score. The ability for the walking dead to get around will lead to higher infection rates.

3. Fewest hardware stores. Chain saws will protect you better than guns (p. 48).

4. Most hospitals. They provide an easy food source for zombies because the weak cannot move as fast.

*Source: Trulia.com

THE ZOMBIE VIRUS: WHY IT IS NOT THAT SCARY

In *Night of the Living Dead*, a zombie virus infects people and turns their brains into worm meal, but could a zombie virus really spread throughout the population?

Viruses are microscopic infectious agents that need a host body to survive. Once they find a host (your body), they invade your cells and inject their genetic material into them. Then they replicate and invade more cells. That's when you start spewing snot or, if you are really unlucky, get the bubonic

plague's telltale pus-filled sores in your groin and armpits. (Yes, the plague still exists.) Viruses are behind some deadly diseases. Sometimes these infectious diseases become so widespread that they infect whole communities. When this happens, it is called an epidemic. Some infectious diseases spread throughout the world. When that happens, it is called a **pandemic**. Whether an epidemic or a pandemic, the zombie virus has one goal—to infect as many people as possible.

1. ZOMBIES BITE

In most movies, a zombie virus is spread through a bite. Unless you are a tiny insect, biting is not the quickest way to spread a virus. For example, rabies is a dangerous disease often spread though a bite, but it cannot spread rapidly.

2. ZOMBIES ARE GROSS

Viruses have a period of time where the person doesn't show symptoms and may not know they are infected. This is called the **incubation period**. For example, the incubation period for rabies can be years. One day, you might be playing with your dog and . . . bam! He starts foaming at the mouth and attacks you.

The incubation is much shorter with a zombie virus. In most movies, the person is bitten and then wakes up a few minutes later as a zombie. Now, are you really going to share a drinking glass with your best friend if his lips are falling off into the glass? In order for a disease to spread effectively, there must be that sneaky incubation period when you don't know someone is infected.

3. HUMANS ARE SMARTER THAN ZOMBIES

Humans are really good at eliminating the enemy, especially when they have science on their side. Brainless monsters don't stand a chance against angry humans.

In 2016, *MythBusters* tested three zombie-killing weapons—a pistol, an ax, and a chain saw. The chain saw resulted in the most kills.

4. ZOMBIES HAVE TOO MANY ENEMIES

A dead body decomposes in approximately forty days, but add heat and humidity and you have a zombie's head rolling off like a scoop of ice cream onto a hot pavement. First, there is the bacteria attacking that delicious zombie flesh, along with maggots, blowflies, and flesh flies. Those insects would start with the moist bits—the eye sockets and eardrums. Then vultures can gobble up a body in less than two hours, followed by wolves, bears, and other wild animals that are going to love the immediate food supply. Even if a zombie makes it to forty days, that is a short enough time period for most people to hide in their basement and wait it out before the zombie is reduced to a pile of rotting flesh.

FLESH FLIES

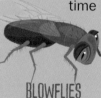

BLOWFLIES

THE ZOMBIE VIRUS LIFE CYCLE

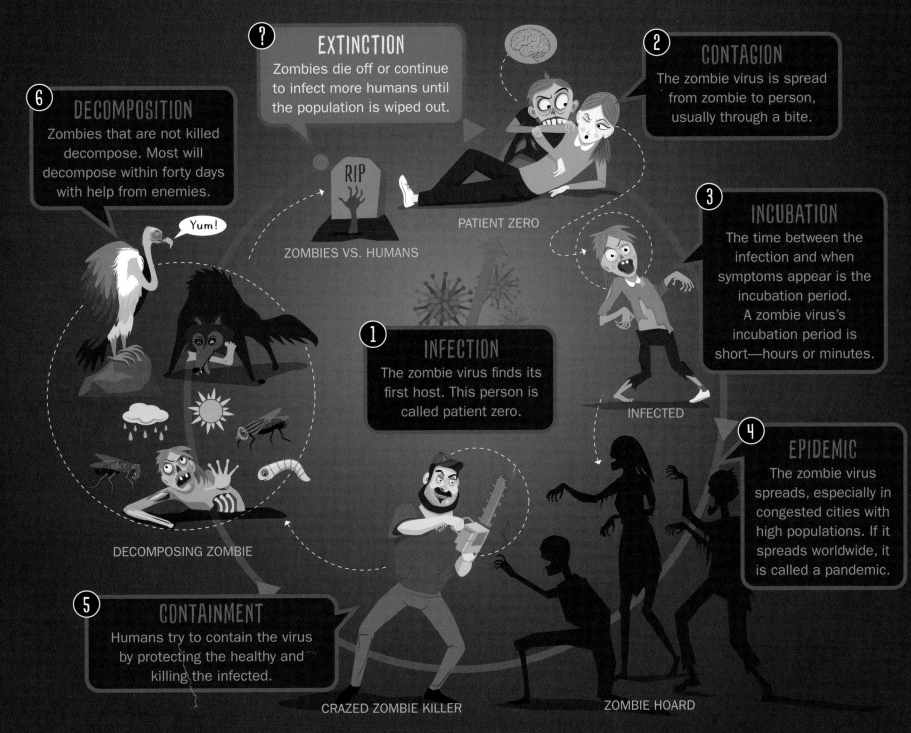

EXTINCTION ⁇
Zombies die off or continue to infect more humans until the population is wiped out.

2 CONTAGION
The zombie virus is spread from zombie to person, usually through a bite.

6 DECOMPOSITION
Zombies that are not killed decompose. Most will decompose within forty days with help from enemies.

Yum!

RIP

ZOMBIES VS. HUMANS

PATIENT ZERO

3 INCUBATION
The time between the infection and when symptoms appear is the incubation period. A zombie virus's incubation period is short—hours or minutes.

1 INFECTION
The zombie virus finds its first host. This person is called patient zero.

INFECTED

DECOMPOSING ZOMBIE

4 EPIDEMIC
The zombie virus spreads, especially in congested cities with high populations. If it spreads worldwide, it is called a pandemic.

5 CONTAINMENT
Humans try to contain the virus by protecting the healthy and killing the infected.

CRAZED ZOMBIE KILLER

ZOMBIE HOARD

If you become a zombie, you will need to stay zombified until someone finds a cure. Follow these nutritional tips to extend your zombie life:

1. EAT FEWER CALORIES.

Assuming that your metabolism has slowed down because, well . . . you are dead, you would require fewer than the average two thousand to twenty-five hundred calories needed by a moderately active human. But unlike humans, zombies have one problem when it comes to digestion—they can't poop. Digestion simply doesn't work for dead people. This means that anything you eat is going to build up in what is left of your stomach until it explodes. Your best bet to extend your miserable zombie existence is to avoid calorie-rich human bits. (See the diagram on the following page to help you choose the best cuts.)

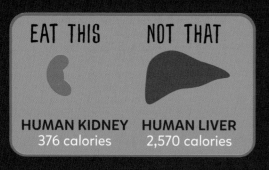

EAT THIS

NOT THAT

HUMAN KIDNEY
376 calories

HUMAN LIVER
2,570 calories

2. EAT RAW.

Cooking increases the calories in meat. To consume fewer calories, always eat your human raw.

3. SKIP THE BRAINS.

If you want to survive as a zombie, you must find healthier alternatives to eating brains. Brains are not only very high in fat, but eating them can also cause a deadly disease called **kuru**. Kuru occurs when someone eats pathogenic proteins inside human brain tissue called **prions**. The disease degrades neurological functions leading to uncontrollable muscle jerks, difficulty walking, headaches, and eventually death. Because you already have that dead look in your eyes, you don't want to eat anything that would make things worse.

4. DON'T EAT GRANDMA.

Always choose to eat younger people instead of older people. Young meat is tender, while old-people meat is too tough and stringy for your rotting teeth to bite.

TIP: DON'T EAT OLD PEOPLE. THEY ARE BOTH FEISTY AND HARD TO CHEW.

ZOMBIE CALORIE COUNTER

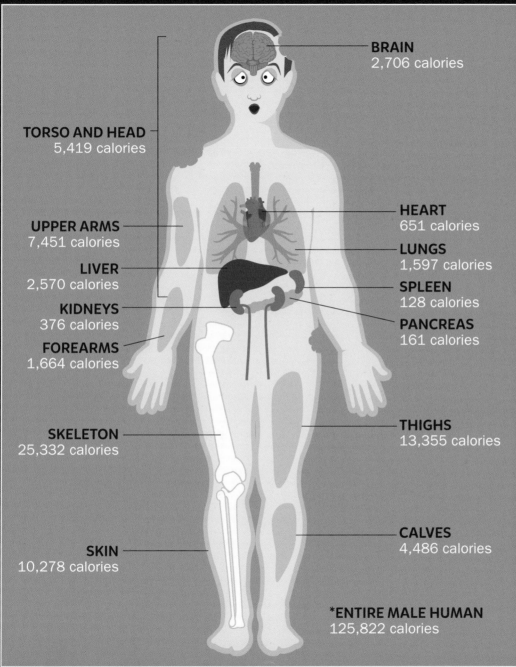

BRAIN
2,706 calories

TORSO AND HEAD
5,419 calories

UPPER ARMS
7,451 calories

HEART
651 calories

LUNGS
1,597 calories

LIVER
2,570 calories

SPLEEN
128 calories

KIDNEYS
376 calories

PANCREAS
161 calories

FOREARMS
1,664 calories

SKELETON
25,332 calories

THIGHS
13,355 calories

CALVES
4,486 calories

SKIN
10,278 calories

*ENTIRE MALE HUMAN
125,822 calories

No one likes zombies because they eat people, and since they were once human, many consider that to be cannibalism. **Cannibalism** is the practice of eating the flesh of your own species. It may seem pretty disgusting to eat people, but our ancestor *Homo antecessor* practiced cannibalism about one million years ago. Scientists originally thought prehistoric humans ate one another because they were just really hungry and needed the calories to survive, but human flesh is really fatty and not that nutritious. If you were to eat an entire male, you would consume 125,822 calories, or the equivalent of approximately 233 Big Macs. That may seem like a lot of calories, but it is not many calories when you consider a boar is 324,000 calories and a woolly mammoth is 3,600,000 calories (6,545 Big Macs)! Clearly, killing and eating a woolly mammoth would be more effective in preventing starvation.

One theory for cannibalistic behavior is that when a person died, prehistoric humans might have felt it was wasteful to not eat the person. Another theory is that cannibalism could have been practiced as part of a sacred ritual, sort of like eating people instead of cake on your birthday. Unfortunately, we may never know why our ancestors ate one another. Maybe some were infected with the zombie virus.

HOW TO SURVIVE A ZOMBIE ATTACK

Many zombie survival guides recommend you have dangerous weapons to fight the invading zombie hoards. Since most of my young zombie fighters don't know how to wield a samurai sword or swing a machete, the following are less bloody ways to survive a zombie apocalypse.

1. WAIT IT OUT.
Zombies have terrible attention spans. Even if one spots you, if you hide, it will eventually give up the hunt and get distracted by another shiny, fleshy thing. The worst thing you can do is call attention to yourself by running or screaming like a terrified baby.

2. FIND A ZOMBIE-FREE ZONE.
Go to the top floor of a building. Most zombies cannot climb stairs, nor can they work the buttons on elevators. Zombies are also horrible swimmers, so islands and oil platforms make excellent locales to wait out the zombie apocalypse.

TIP: ACT LIKE A ZOMBIE.

3. WEAR A HELMET.
The same device that protects your brain from bike accidents will also protect you from a zombie bite. Zombies' decomposing mouths are not strong enough to bite through a helmet. Zombies also are not smart enough to undo the strap.

4. AVOID SHOPPING MALLS.
Or anywhere else where mass hysteria might occur. Have you seen what Black Friday shoppers will do the day after Thanksgiving to score a discounted big-screen TV? That scary, muscled guy fighting to get the last can of Spam is far more dangerous than a zombie.

5. ACT LIKE A ZOMBIE.
If you have ever watched any zombie movies, you know they will tear the flesh off an innocent child, gnaw through your grandma's bones, and slurp up every last drop of human blood. But eat their own brethren . . . well, that's just savage. Zombies never eat other zombies. You can use this knowledge to disguise your tasty flesh. Practice your zombie shuffle and aimless stare daily. If that doesn't work, you can stop showering to mimic that rotting flesh stink.

YOUR ZOMBIE PREPAREDNESS KIT

Concern about zombies was so great that in 2013, the Centers for Disease Control and Prevention (CDC) released a zombie preparedness kit. Here is what the CDC recommends that you have to survive a zombie apocalypse (or other pandemic):

WATER
1 gallon (3.8 L) per person, per day

MULTIPURPOSE SUPPLIES
wrench, pliers, duct tape, scissors, matches

FIRST AID KIT
a seven-day supply of medications, a whistle, antibiotic ointment, bandages, face masks, gloves

FLASHLIGHTS
with extra batteries

MAPS

DOCUMENTS
copies of the medication list, proof of address, deed/lease to home, passports, birth certificates, insurance policies

EMERGENCY BLANKET
with extra clothes and one sleeping bag per person

EXTRA CASH

RADIO
battery-powered or hand-crank

PERSONAL ITEMS
soap, toothbrush, toothpaste, toilet paper, bleach

FOOD
nonperishable items (minimum three-day supply)

CELL PHONE
with charger

Whether zombies or another disaster hits, preparing an emergency kit is vital for your family's survival. Remember, you may be without food, water, or electricity for days.

TIP: Review your disaster plan with family members.

REAL MONSTERS: CREATURES USING ZOMBIE MIND CONTROL

Creatures that take over your brain and force you to do their bidding may sound like a sci-fi movie, but the following parasites are capable of some disturbing mind control:

CHARLOTTE'S ZOMBIE WEB

Spiders weave several types of webs to catch prey: the sheet web, orb web, tangle web, and funnel web, but none is more terrifying than the zombie web. When the wasp *Reclinervellus nielseni* encounters the spider *Cyclosa argenteoalba*, it lays an egg on its back. This alters the spider's brain and gets the infected spider to tear down its usual spiral-shaped web and spin an entirely different web—a strong, hanging web with few spokes that won't catch any flies but is perfectly suited to support the wasp's cocoon. Once the wasp's babies develop into larvae, the wasp larvae thank the spider by gobbling it up. Scientists still do not know what the wasp injects into the spider's brain to make it do its bidding, but it certainly is a neat trick.

THE ZOM-BEES

With vampire mites, pesticides, and nutritional deficiencies already wreaking havoc on honeybee populations, having to deal with parasitic flies turning them into zombies is a bit much. The fly, *Apocephalus borealis*, pierces the abdomen of the bee and deposits its eggs inside it. Once infected, worker bees then forget about foraging for nectar and pollen and instead walk aimlessly in circles . . . like zombies. Most eerily, instead

Go toward the light...

of collecting pollen during the day, they swarm at night and circle lights until they drop dead. The fly larvae then slowly eat the bees from the inside out until they emerge through the honeybees' abdomens like an alien birth scene.

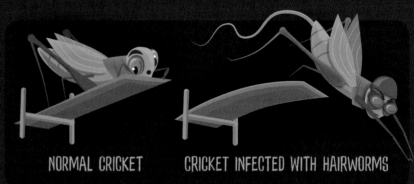

NORMAL CRICKET   CRICKET INFECTED WITH HAIRWORMS

SUICIDAL CRICKETS

Suicidal crickets is not just the name of my next book, it also describes the self-destructive behavior of crickets infected with hairworms.* The hairworm larva infects an unsuspecting cricket by burrowing through its stomach. Once it reaches adulthood, the hairworm must live out its remaining life in water. It has only one problem—crickets are terrible swimmers and generally avoid water. To get the cricket into the water, the hairworm takes control of the cricket's brain and makes the cricket think it is suddenly an Olympic diver. The infected cricket then cannonballs into water, plummeting to its watery end. Once the cricket drowns, the hairworm emerges from the cricket's gut and swims off to find a mate and complete the cycle again.

---

*If that is the title of my next children's book, then I have figured out a way to use parasites to control my editor's mind.

your cat lick your face. *Toxoplasma gondii (T. gondii)* is a parasite that can infect any warm-blooded animal but prefers to make baby *T. Gondii*s inside a cat's gut. In its quest to reproduce inside a cat, *T. Gondii* infects mice and rewires their brains to become attracted to the smell of cat urine. An infected mouse then seeks out the cat urine and, therefore, the cat. The cat, of course, does not share this attraction and eats the infected mouse. Once inside the cat's gut, *T. Gondii* reproduces. Then the cat sheds the parasite's tiny eggs in its feces.

Humans can sometimes ingest these eggs when they clean a cat's litter box, play in contaminated soil and then

infected, most people do not feel different other than brief flu-like symptoms . . . at least not at first. But this parasitic infection has been linked to several mental disorders, including schizophrenia, impulsivity, and even reckless driving. In one study, men infected with *T. gondii* were more likely to report that they liked the smell of cat urine. The medical community is still divided on the connection between mental illness and *T. gondii* infections. Some doctors claim that it is all hype, but that's probably just the zombie parasite controlling their brains.

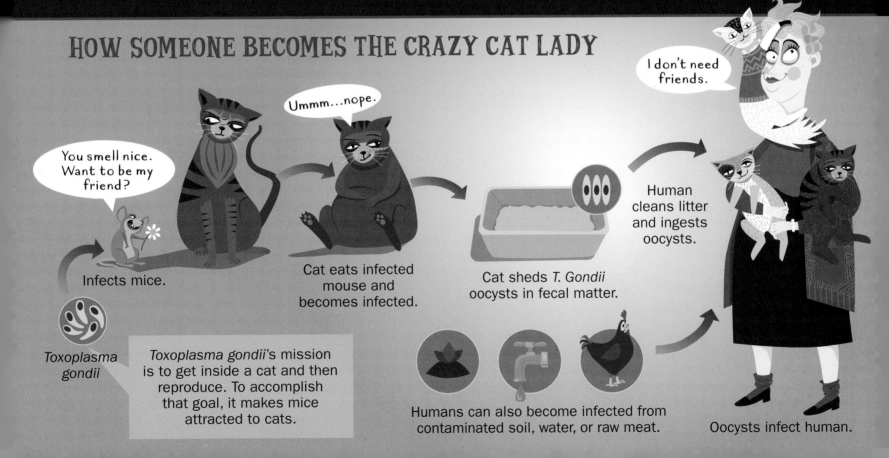

HOW SOMEONE BECOMES THE CRAZY CAT LADY

You smell nice. Want to be my friend?

Ummm...nope.

I don't need friends.

Infects mice.

Toxoplasma gondii

Toxoplasma gondii's mission is to get inside a cat and then reproduce. To accomplish that goal, it makes mice attracted to cats.

Cat eats infected mouse and becomes infected.

Cat sheds *T. Gondii* oocysts in fecal matter.

Human cleans litter and ingests oocysts.

Humans can also become infected from contaminated soil, water, or raw meat.

Oocysts infect human.

THE LEADING MAN

Legend has it that when actress Fay Wray was asked to play the role of King Kong's love interest, she was promised the "tallest, darkest leading man in Hollywood." She would only later find out that her tall, dark leading man was really a monster ape.

At the time, gorillas were pretty scary. Nineteenth-century explorers told tales of hairy men with incredible strength who stole women, but no one knew what they were. It wasn't until 1902 that the first mountain gorilla was discovered. Even then, the public was slow to learn about gorillas partly because they often died in captivity. The first exhibit of a gorilla in an American zoo was not until 1911. With the public growing curious about apes, *King Kong* premiered in 1933 to sold-out audiences and grossed $10 million in the United States (a large amount for a movie during the Great Depression). Today the film is considered by many critics to be the greatest horror film of all time, but how much of King Kong is based on reality?

DID BEAUTY OR MATH KILL THE BEAST?

Movies would like you to believe that monsters can grow to humongous sizes, but most monsters would get crushed under their own weight if they got that big. The problem is not the size, but the **volume**—the amount of space the monster occupies.

For example, if you wanted to calculate the area of a 2-inch square, you would multiply the length of one side by the length of the other, or L^2, and get an area of 4 **(A)**. But objects are not one-sided. They exist in three dimensions. So we also need to calculate the volume to get a true measurement of its size. To calculate the volume of a cube, we would multiply its Length × Length × Length, or L^3, to get 8 **(B)**.

Now what if we doubled the size of our cube? The new length of one of its sides is now 4 so its area would be 16 (4 × 4), but its volume is 64 (4 × 4 × 4) **(C)**. The volume increases at a much greater rate than the area does. This is a principal in mathematics called the **square-cube law**. This law states that as an object's area gets larger, its volume increases in direct proportion but at a greater rate.

KING KONG'S ACHING JOINTS

A silverback gorilla is approximately 6 feet tall (1.8 m) and 350 pounds (159 kg). Kong is 24 feet tall (7.3 m), or roughly four times the height of a gorilla. Because Kong is about the same shape as a gorilla except four times as large, we know from the square-cube law that as his area increases, his volume increases at a greater rate.

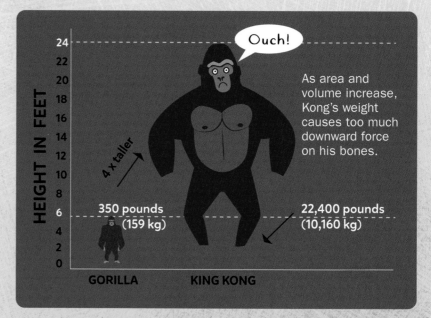

As area and volume increase, Kong's weight causes too much downward force on his bones.

All three-dimensional objects are subject to the square-cube law. Not even movie monsters can escape it. Unfortunately for King Kong, his greater volume also increases his weight proportionally. There comes a point at which the area of the monster's bones and muscles cannot support the force of his weight. His bones would break before he got one floor up the Empire State Building.

WHAT IS WEIGHT?
Weight is the force of gravity on an object.

DOUBLE ITS SIZE →

A
2
2
AREA = L^2
2 X 2 = 4

B
2
2
2
VOLUME = L^3
2 X 2 X 2 = 8

C
2
2
2
4
4
4
AREA = 4 X 4 = 16
VOLUME = 4 X 4 X 4 = 64

Calculate the area of a 2-inch square and the volume of a 2-inch cube

If we double its size, the volume increases at a greater rate than its area.

MATH MAKES MONSTERS MISERABLE

With the exception of some whales and sharks, dinosaurs are the largest animals to ever live. Getting so big requires thick but light bones to support the body, similar to how we use strong but lightweight materials in buildings. They also have to have a strong enough heart to pump blood throughout the body. And lastly, they must have enough food (see p. 61).

But even when these factors are met, we know from the square-cube law that every living thing has a size limit. Large dinosaurs such as triceratops got stress fractures (tiny breaks in their bones) most likely for this very reason—they simply grew too heavy for their bones to support them. Dinosaurs like *Tyrannosaurus rex* broke bones if they turned too fast and were so bulky that they could only manage a fast walk of about 12 miles (19 km) per hour. You have probably experienced the pitfalls of the square-cube law at the beach. Build a sandcastle too tall and it will collapse under its weight (unless you change the building material to something lighter, stronger, or both).

This is not my chapter, but I hate math too.

The square-cube law also makes Godzilla impossible.

Triceratops had stress fractures in their bones due to their weight.

I can't help you T. My knees are killing me!

T. *rex* sometimes toppled over if it turned too fast.

Curse you, square-cube law!

Sorry, guys, I can't even move. The movie directors made me too big.

THE BIGGER THEY ARE, THE HARDER THEY FALL

In the original *King Kong* movie, the monster climbs to the top of the Empire State Building as he fights off attacking planes. Exhausted and heartbroken from being rejected by his lady love, he eventually falls to his death. New Yorkers on the street gape at the bloodied mass of fur that has become Kong's body. In real life . . . onlookers might want to stay clear of Kong's fall.

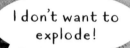

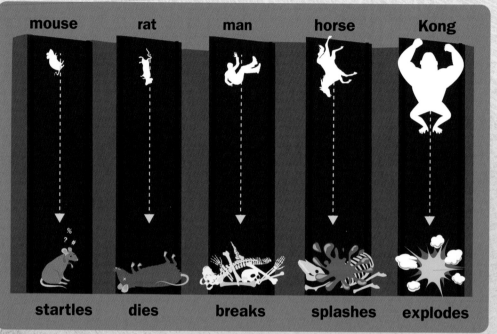

Dropped down a 1,000-yard (914 m) mine shaft

Biologist John Burdon Sanderson Haldane explained the square-cube law by using the following analogy: "You can drop a mouse down a thousand-yard [914 m] mine shaft; and, on arriving at the bottom, it gets a slight shock and walks away, provided that the ground is fairly soft. A rat is killed, a man is broken, a horse splashes."

THAT'S BANANAS

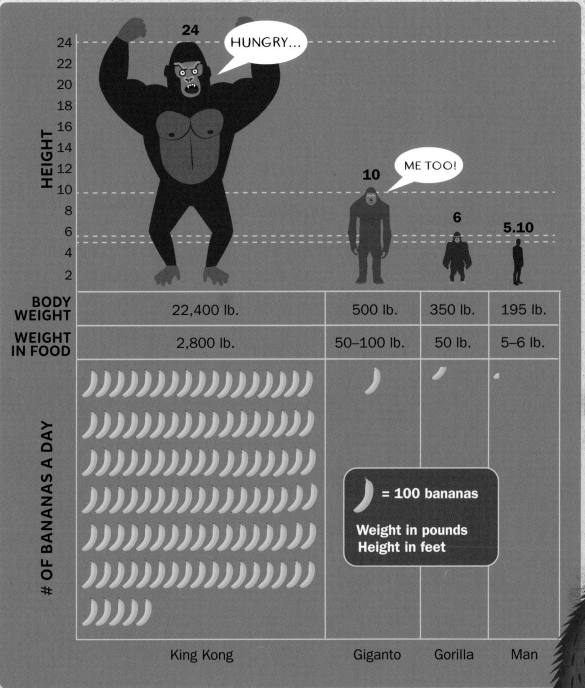

	King Kong	Giganto	Gorilla	Man
HEIGHT	24	10	6	5.10
BODY WEIGHT	22,400 lb.	500 lb.	350 lb.	195 lb.
WEIGHT IN FOOD	2,800 lb.	50–100 lb.	50 lb.	5–6 lb.

Speech bubbles: HUNGRY... / ME TOO!

) = 100 bananas

Weight in pounds
Height in feet

King Kong is hungry. An average 300- to 400-pound (136 to 181 kg) male gorilla eats 50 pounds (23 kg) of food per day, or one-eighth of its body weight. If a 22,400-pound (10,160 kg) gorilla ate just one-eighth of its body weight, he would need 2,800 pounds (1,270 kg) of food, or 10,769 bananas per day. Even if Kong ate small children to offset his plant diet, he would still have trouble finding enough food (especially on an island). The largest known ape was *Gigantopithecus blacki*, or Giganto, (p. 108). At 10 feet (3 m) tall and 500 pounds (227 kg), scientists believe *Gigantopithecus* went extinct because it couldn't find enough food to survive.

Speech bubble: People are chewy!

ARE YOU STRONGER THAN A DUNG BEETLE?

Just because an animal is monster-sized, that doesn't mean it is monster strong. The following are examples of how body size relates to true strength:

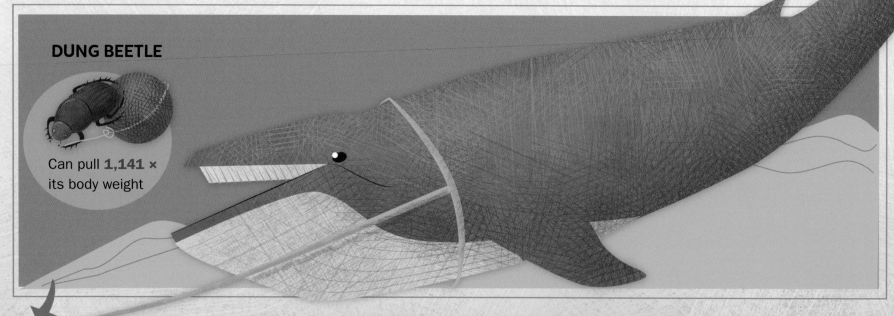

DUNG BEETLE

Can pull **1,141 ×** its body weight

If an average 195-pound (88 kg) man could pull **1,141 ×** his own weight, he could pull a blue whale.

I may be small, but I am strong for my size.

Because of the square-cube law, smaller animals have more relative muscle strength than larger animals. An ant's ratio of muscle to mass allows it to lift fifty times its body weight.

LEAFCUTTER ANT

Can lift **50 ×** its body weight

If an average 195-pound (88 kg) man lifted **50 ×** his body weight, he could lift a three-quarter-ton truck.

RHINO BEETLE

Can lift **100 ×** its body weight

If a woman could lift **100 ×** her body weight, she could lift three white rhinos.

AFRICAN CROWNED EAGLE

This graphic doesn't even make sense? I can't fly or lift a tiger.

Can carry **4 ×** its body weight

If a man could lift **4 ×** his body weight, he could carry a large tiger.

AFRICAN FOREST ELEPHANT

I can only support a few hundred pounds on my back so please stop riding me!

Can carry **10 percent** of its body weight

If a woman could lift only **10 percent** of her body weight, she would barely be able to lift a watermelon.

I can't even lift this tiny movie star.

As animals get bigger, they do get stronger, but their strength does not increase in direct proportion to their mass. This means a big animal like an elephant can lift a lot of weight, but it's not a lot of weight in relation to its size.

THE REAL SKULL ISLAND

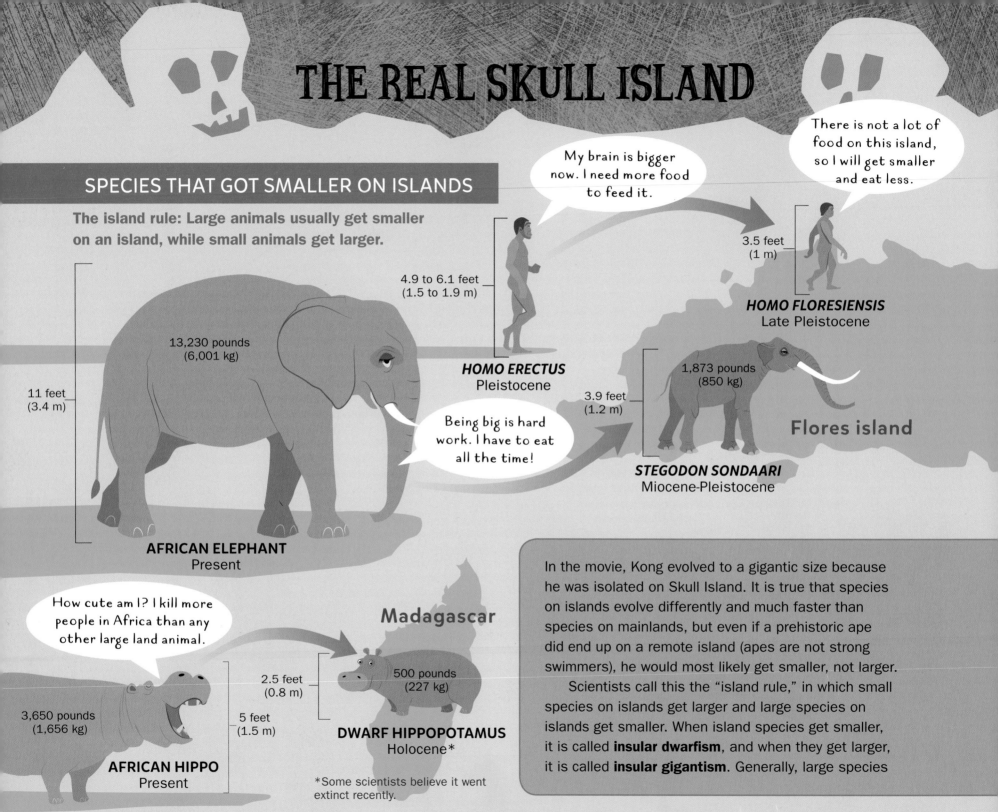

SPECIES THAT GOT SMALLER ON ISLANDS

The island rule: Large animals usually get smaller on an island, while small animals get larger.

My brain is bigger now. I need more food to feed it.

There is not a lot of food on this island, so I will get smaller and eat less.

4.9 to 6.1 feet
(1.5 to 1.9 m)

3.5 feet
(1 m)

HOMO ERECTUS
Pleistocene

HOMO FLORESIENSIS
Late Pleistocene

11 feet
(3.4 m)

13,230 pounds
(6,001 kg)

Being big is hard work. I have to eat all the time!

3.9 feet
(1.2 m)

1,873 pounds
(850 kg)

Flores island

STEGODON SONDAARI
Miocene-Pleistocene

AFRICAN ELEPHANT
Present

How cute am I? I kill more people in Africa than any other large land animal.

Madagascar

500 pounds
(227 kg)

2.5 feet
(0.8 m)

5 feet
(1.5 m)

3,650 pounds
(1,656 kg)

DWARF HIPPOPOTAMUS
Holocene*

AFRICAN HIPPO
Present

*Some scientists believe it went extinct recently.

In the movie, Kong evolved to a gigantic size because he was isolated on Skull Island. It is true that species on islands evolve differently and much faster than species on mainlands, but even if a prehistoric ape did end up on a remote island (apes are not strong swimmers), he would most likely get smaller, not larger.

Scientists call this the "island rule," in which small species on islands get larger and large species on islands get smaller. When island species get smaller, it is called **insular dwarfism**, and when they get larger, it is called **insular gigantism**. Generally, large species

SPECIES THAT GOT LARGER ON ISLANDS

I may have eaten a few hobbits

or at least a few large rats

or maybe some hobbit babies.

6 feet (1.8 m)

5 feet (1.5 m)

44 inches (112 cm)

MARABOU STORK
Present

WHITE STORK
Present

16 to 17.5 inches (41 to 44 cm)

I will swim to New York City and terrorize people. Then I will get a movie deal!

LEPTOPTILOS ROBUSTUS
Pleistocene

FLORES GIANT RAT
Present

24 inches (61 cm)

I ate the Easter Bunny.

...Gulp.

How did I get on an island? I can't even swim?

I can swim!

8 inches (20 cm)

13 to 16 inches (33 to 41 cm)

Minorca

BROWN RAT
Present

MEGAPRIMATUS KONG
Present

NURALAGUS REX
Late Miocene to Middle Pliocene

DOMESTIC RABBIT
Present

get smaller because they do not need to cover large distances of land to find food on an island, nor do they have as much competition or predators.

One example of insular dwarfism is on the island of Flores in Indonesia. Flores was once inhabited by some very short people. *Homo floresiensis* (nicknamed the hobbit) was about 3.5 feet (1 m) tall and lived as recently as fifty thousand years ago. Scientists speculate that *Homo floresiensis* was smaller because there were few predators and less nutrients on Flores. We still are not certain how the hobbit is related to modern humans, but it most likely

evolved from one of our ape ancestors, *Homo erectus*.

In contrast, Flores also has some freakishly large bugs, rats the size of cats, and storks that were more likely to eat babies than deliver them. One rat called the Flores giant rat even still exists. Insects, rats, and small mammals have one thing in common—even on an island, there are a lot of them. Scientists speculate that small animals need to get larger because increasing in size gives them a competitive edge over a more abundant population. So while being attacked by a giant ape may be all Hollywood drama, being attacked by a giant rat is totally possible.

MEGAPRIMATUS KONG

In the 1933 movie, Kong is a prehistoric ape called *Megaprimatus kong*. Directors modeled Kong to look and act like a silverback gorilla, but Kong doesn't always play his role like a true gorilla. Which are the true characteristics of gorillas? *The answers are on the following page.*

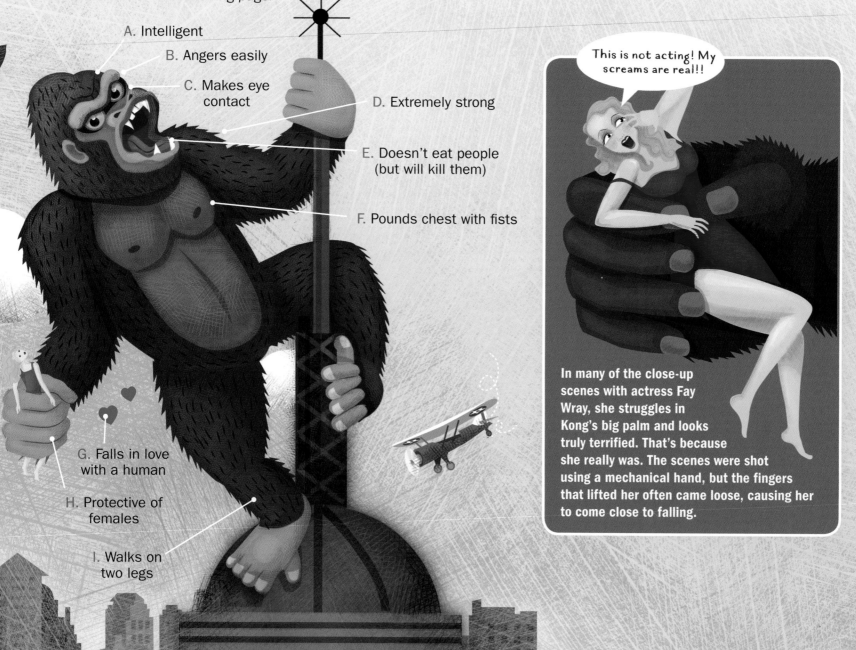

A. Intelligent

B. Angers easily

C. Makes eye contact

D. Extremely strong

E. Doesn't eat people (but will kill them)

F. Pounds chest with fists

G. Falls in love with a human

H. Protective of females

I. Walks on two legs

This is not acting! My screams are real!!

In many of the close-up scenes with actress Fay Wray, she struggles in Kong's big palm and looks truly terrified. That's because she really was. The scenes were shot using a mechanical hand, but the fingers that lifted her often came loose, causing her to come close to falling.

ANSWERS: THE REAL *GORILLA BERINGEI*

The first silverback gorillas were not discovered until 1902, so we can forgive movie directors in 1933 for Kong's sometimes un-apelike characteristics. (Later movies corrected some of the inaccuracies.)

A. TRUE

Gorillas are extremely intelligent and can even be taught to communicate with humans by using sign language.

B. TRUE

You don't want to anger a 350-pound (159 kg) gorilla. Gorillas are generally very gentle, but just like people, if you anger one . . . it will attack.

C. FALSE

You might not want to stare a gorilla in the eye. Unlike humans, gorillas interpret prolonged eye contact as a showdown (looking away is a sign of submission). One zoo even had visitors wear special eye goggles that disguised their eyes to prevent the gorillas from getting mad.

D. TRUE

Gorillas can lift ten times their body weight.

E. TRUE

Gorillas are mostly herbivores (plant eaters), but they eat some insects, ants, and termites too. Gorillas do not eat meat.

F. FALSE

Gorillas beat their chests with cupped hands, not fists. They do this to show their dominance, declare a victory, or sometimes just to get their kids to behave.

G. TRUE

Believe it or not, gorillas often flirt with their caretakers by pursing their lips and offering small gifts.

H. TRUE

Just like Kong, male gorillas are extremely protective of their females and will even fight to the death for a mate.

I. FALSE

Gorillas use their knuckles and their feet to remain upright.

Gorillas sometimes get crushes on humans.

♥

TRUE OR FALSE? Humans share 99 percent of our DNA with chimps and 98 percent with gorillas.

Answer: True

A gorilla can lift 10× its body weight.

WEREWOLVES

Crack. Snap. Pop. Bones push their way through stretched skin. Hair sprouts out in angry tufts. Eyes flash a sickly yellow. The hard angles of a snarling mouth break free from their human form, and in one painful yet graceful arch, the creature exhales and lets out a mournful howl. Man has become beast.

In movies, a werewolf's transformation is one of the most gruesome scenes. Many of these werewolf characteristics were invented by the first werewolf movies, such as turning into a werewolf when the moon is full, spreading the curse from a werewolf bite, and the poisoning of werewolves from wolfsbane. But centuries before Hollywood transformed actors into hairy monsters, werewolves were not just fictional monsters howling at the moon. They were a very real danger.

During the sixteenth century in France and Switzerland, it was believed that a witch turned into a wolf to dine on her helpless victims. This mythical ability was called **lycanthropy**, and it was such a real threat that accused werewolves were hunted down and put on trial alongside accused witches.

These early werewolves didn't need a full moon to become a beast. They simply turned their skin inside out. Consequently, werewolf interrogators often peeled back the skin of a suspected werewolf with red-hot pincers or cut off arms and legs to take a peek inside. All this skin-peeling torture caused many people to confess to being a werewolf, and these confessions only made the fear spread.

It didn't help matters that wolf attacks in Europe were a serious problem. Wolves attacked at night, killing livestock and sometimes small children. From 1764 to 1767, approximately one hundred people (mostly children and women) were killed by a supposed werewolf in Southern France called the Beast of Gévaudan. No one knows who or what the beast was, but suspects include a wolf-dog hybrid, a rabid wolf, a hyena, a lion, or a serial killer dressed in animal skins. If you asked the folks living during that time, they would have sworn it was a werewolf.

In countries that lacked wolves, shape-shifters took other forms. The children of North Africa and the Horn of Africa feared the dreaded werehyena, while China's kids were on the lookout for the werefox, which kept her bushy tail even in human form.

WEREWOLVES ARE JUST LIKE US

Humans and werewolves share several traits. Can you guess which ones?

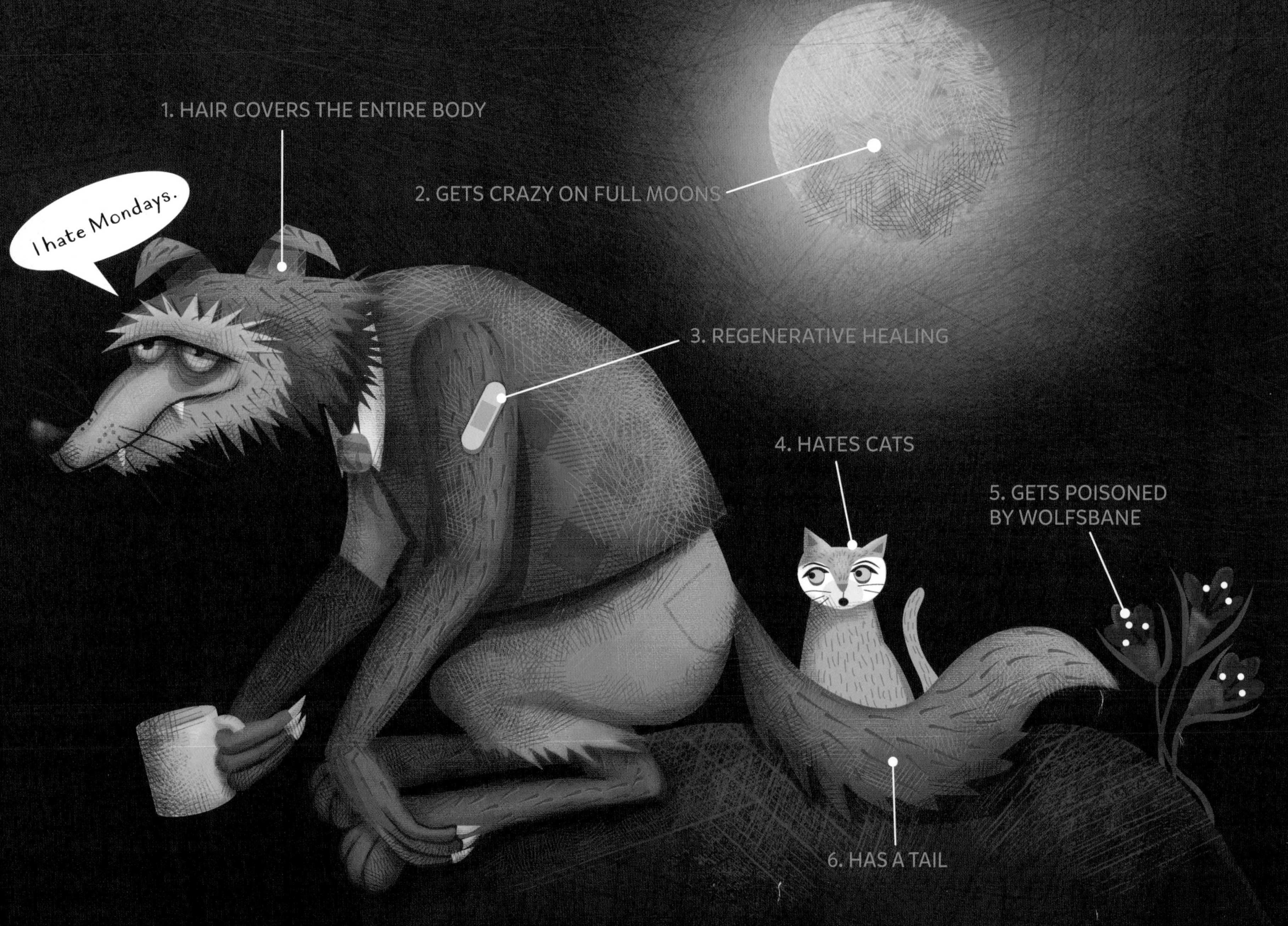

1. HAIR COVERS THE ENTIRE BODY

2. GETS CRAZY ON FULL MOONS

3. REGENERATIVE HEALING

4. HATES CATS

5. GETS POISONED BY WOLFSBANE

6. HAS A TAIL

I hate Mondays.

ANSWERS

1. HAIR: WEREWOLVES AND HUMANS

When you were inside your mother's womb, you were covered with hair. Hair on your back. Hair on your stomach. Hair on your face. You even had hair sprouting out of your ears. All babies look like fuzzy little beasts at one point. This soft, downy hair is called **lanugo**, and it is believed to help regulate the baby's body temperature while in the womb. Lanugo typically falls off at about the eighth or ninth month of pregnancy (babies actually swallow the hair with the amniotic fluid). Some babies, especially premature babies, are born with lanugo still covering their bodies. Despite the different names, hair and fur are the exact same thing. They both are made of a fibrous protein called **keratin**. A werewolf's fur is a bit different from human hair because a werewolf has a dense undercoat made of finer hair and a top coat of denser, coarser hair. Werewolves shed this undercoat during the warmer months.

2. FULL MOON: WEREWOLVES ONLY

Ask any healthcare professional or police officer and they will swear the full moon makes people wacky. Even the word *lunacy*—"the state of insanity"—comes from *lunar*, meaning "resembling the moon." But although a full moon may cause a werewolf to turn, studies have shown it does not lead to increased levels of violence, deaths, births, or any other absurdities in humans.

The full moon does affect animals, but that may be only because there is a giant spotlight on their habitat.

For example, many animals are not as active on full moon nights because it is harder to hide from predators under the light of the moon. Conversely, lions don't hunt as much on full moons, most likely because they instinctively know that their prey hides when there is a lot of moonlight.

You may need to hide from a werewolf on a full moon night, but not a wolf. Wolves howl the most at sunrise and sunset, usually because they are trying to locate their buddies, not because they are hunting through the night.

3. HEALING: WEREWOLVES AND HUMANS

What if every time you fell down and cut yourself, the wound healed within hours? In the movies, werewolves have this ability, but believe it or not, humans also have extraordinary self-repair mechanisms that have baffled scientists for generations. In one case, a man had an incurable tumor and was told he had months to live. Thankfully, his doctor knew of a new drug on the market with an amazing success rate and convinced the man it would cure him. Within weeks, the man's tumor shrunk and he got better. He thanked his doctor, grateful that science had found a cure. But his doctor had tricked him. The "cure" was nothing but salt water.

When people get better from a fake pill, it is called the **placebo effect**. Doctors still don't know why placebos work, but they suspect it is because when you are told you will get better, your body releases feel-good hormones called endorphins that help the body heal. Even something as simple as laughter can speed healing.

4. HATES CATS: MOSTLY WEREWOLVES

It is true that some humans don't care for cats, but werewolves have a special dislike for felines that goes back millions of years. The rivalry started during the Eocene era, about 55.8 to 33.9 million years ago, when felids (early cats) arrived in North America from Asia and started to compete for the same food sources with canids (early dogs and wolves). In this prehistoric smackdown between dog vs. cat, cats came out the victor for one very catlike reason—they were sneaky. Aside from their retractable claws, sharp teeth, powerful limbs, and obvious superiority complex, cats are **ambush hunters**—they lie in wait and then pounce on prey. Dogs, on the other hand, evolved to hunt in packs and run down prey over long distances. All that panting is much more work than waiting for your dinner to cross your path. As a result, cats killed more prey and used up more of the available food sources. Without food, over twenty dog species went extinct while cats survived. So, if you ever see a dog (or werewolf) chasing a cat, know they are just trying to even the score.

WHY WEREWOLVES (AND DOGS) HATE CATS
**The ancestors of early dogs, wolves, and werewolves ran down their prey in packs over long distances.
This required lots of energy and may have made them less efficient hunters.**

5. WOLFSBANE: WEREWOLVES AND HUMANS

In most werewolf legends, a werewolf grows weak and dies if it is around wolfsbane. But wolfsbane, otherwise known as *Aconitum napellus*, is not just werewolf fiction. The ancient Greeks rubbed wolfsbane on their arrows to kill wolves or sometimes used it to poison their enemy's water supply. In medieval times, wolfsbane was part of the "flying ointment" that witches used to make their broomsticks do more than just sweep the floor. (The ointment also caused hallucinations . . . which might make some people think they are flying.) Digesting wolfsbane or even just touching its purple flowers can cause organ failure and eventually death. (The roots are the most poisonous.) In 2014, one gardener in Britain died after handling the deadly plant without protective gloves. The lesson: Don't try to kill a werewolf with poison unless you are an experienced toxicologist.

6. TAIL: WEREWOLVES AND HUMANS

You once had a tail. At about thirty days old, a human fetus has a tail that gets absorbed before birth. Scientists believe

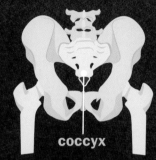

coccyx

The coccyx is what remains of the tail humans once had.

our prehistoric ancestors also had long monkey tails, but through evolution, our tails disappeared. No one really knows why humans lost their tails, but it may have been because once we learned to walk upright, we no longer needed a tail to counterbalance our weight. Humans do still have remnants of this lost tail. At the base of your spine are fused vertebra, called the **coccyx**, or tailbone.

Early cats were ambush hunters. They lay in wait for their prey and pounced. This hunting method required less energy and may be one of the reasons why they were more efficient hunters. Unfortunately, because cats hogged food sources, many dog breeds went extinct.

HOW TO COMMUNICATE WITH A WEREWOLF

Unfortunately, werewolves cannot talk, but just like wolves and dogs, they do use body language to communicate. The following will indicate if a werewolf is mad enough to eat you:

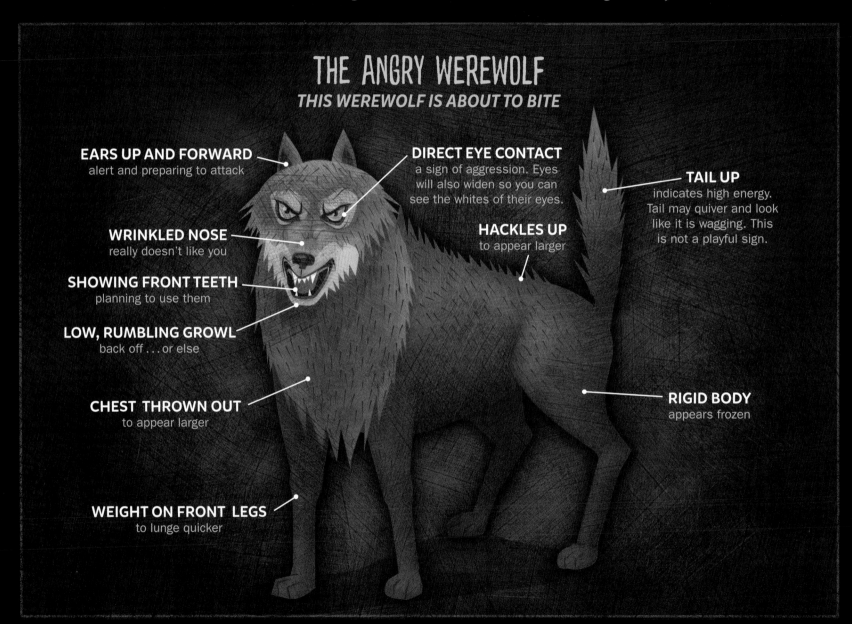

THE ANGRY WEREWOLF
THIS WEREWOLF IS ABOUT TO BITE

EARS UP AND FORWARD
alert and preparing to attack

DIRECT EYE CONTACT
a sign of aggression. Eyes will also widen so you can see the whites of their eyes.

TAIL UP
indicates high energy. Tail may quiver and look like it is wagging. This is not a playful sign.

WRINKLED NOSE
really doesn't like you

HACKLES UP
to appear larger

SHOWING FRONT TEETH
planning to use them

LOW, RUMBLING GROWL
back off . . . or else

CHEST THROWN OUT
to appear larger

RIGID BODY
appears frozen

WEIGHT ON FRONT LEGS
to lunge quicker

Please note: Dogs communicate with the same body language when they are about to bite.

Sometimes a werewolf can't decide if he wants to eat you. Often this werewolf is frightened and will bite only if there is no escape. This werewolf can be just as dangerous.

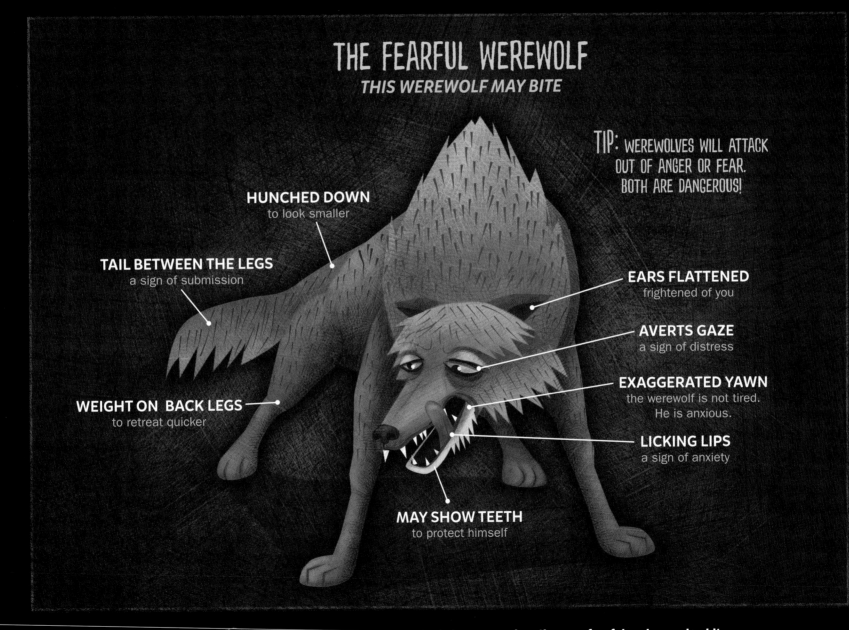

THE FEARFUL WEREWOLF
THIS WEREWOLF MAY BITE

TIP: WEREWOLVES WILL ATTACK OUT OF ANGER OR FEAR. BOTH ARE DANGEROUS!

HUNCHED DOWN
to look smaller

TAIL BETWEEN THE LEGS
a sign of submission

EARS FLATTENED
frightened of you

AVERTS GAZE
a sign of distress

EXAGGERATED YAWN
the werewolf is not tired.
He is anxious.

WEIGHT ON BACK LEGS
to retreat quicker

LICKING LIPS
a sign of anxiety

MAY SHOW TEETH
to protect himself

Please note: Dogs communicate with the same body language when they are fearful and may also bite.

75

HOW TO AVOID A WEREWOLF ATTACK

Most werewolf guides will tell you to arm yourself with axes, knives, crossbows, and guns with silver bullets. Instead of having dangerous weapons in the house, use the following safer tips to avoid a werewolf attack:

1. USE THE PROPER WEREWOLF GREETING.
If a dog greets another dog, it will often stick its nose right in the animal's butt. Werewolves, dogs, and wolves do this not because they like the smell but because they are sifting through the different odors coming from the anal sac. With humans they will stick their nose in the crotch area because it has more sweat glands and therefore has more odors. In fact, they can detect gender, diet, health, and emotional state just from the bouquet of smells wafting out of the crotch. A dog's sense of smell is so great that it can even smell when a diabetic's blood sugar is off and can detect certain cancers.

2. REMAIN CALM.
Do not scream or make any sudden movements. If you seem agitated, a werewolf is more likely to attack. Remember—werewolves, like dogs, can smell fear. When you are frightened, your sweat glands open and produce more body odor, which the werewolf can smell.

3. DO NOT LOOK IT IN THE EYE.
Werewolves have a lot of rage, so your best bet to survive an attack is to not incite the monster's wrath. Eye contact is interpreted as an act of aggression in werewolves, wolves, and dogs.

4. BACK AWAY SLOWLY.
Whatever you do . . . do not run! Running will trigger a predatory response, and the werewolf is bound to plow you down and chew off your arms and legs. Always remember that werewolves (like wolves and dogs) are hunters, so they instinctively want to attack and kill anything that runs away.

Nice wolfy...

TRY TO REMAIN CALM

DO NOT LOOK WEREWOLF IN THE EYE

WEREWOLF MAY TRY TO SMELL YOU

KEEP ARMS BY YOUR SIDE

NEVER FACE WEREWOLF DIRECTLY

BACK AWAY SLOWLY

*Please note: Many of these same techniques can be used to survive wolf and angry dog attacks.

76

HOW TO SURVIVE IF A WEREWOLF ATTACKS

Despite your efforts to communicate politely, some werewolves are jerks and may bite you anyway. Follow these tips to survive:

1. PROTECT YOUR FACE, THROAT, AND CHEST. Roll

onto your stomach, tuck your knees in, and bring your hands to your face to protect it. Keep your hands in a fist to protect your fingers.

2. DO NOT SCREAM. Your screams will only excite the

werewolf more and encourage it to attack you further.

3. TREAT ANY WOUNDS. Seek medical attention

immediately for any wounds. Do not tell doctors or nurses you have been bitten by a werewolf. They will only think you are crazy and call a psychiatrist. Instead, insist you were attacked by a dog or wolf.

4. BECOME EDUCATED. If you have been bitten by a

werewolf, you will now become one every full moon. Reread this chapter to be prepared for the aftermath.

REAL MONSTERS: WHICH BEAST KILLS THE MOST PEOPLE?

- 0 WEREWOLF*
- 3 WOLF
- 10 BROWN BEAR
- 28 COYOTE
- 392 DOG

I am always getting blamed for the werewolf attacks.

Number of deaths in the US between 2005–2016 *Please note: Many werewolf attacks go unreported or are confused with wolf attacks.

CALL THE DOCTOR OR THE WOLF HUNTER?

Throughout history, some people were accused of being a werewolf when they really just had medical problems. Here are some examples of werewolf-like illnesses:

I think I need to start shaving now...

LYCANTHROPY

While pretending to be a dog, cat, or horse can be fun, imagine really believing you are an animal. **Lycanthropy** is a rare mental illness where patients look in the mirror and see only hairy bodies, claws, snouts, and other nonhuman traits. One famous case of possible lycanthropy was a teenage boy named Jean Grenier who in 1603 wore a special wolf pelt he claimed turned him into a werewolf. On his hunts, Grenier also claimed to have "killed dogs and drunk their blood," but he preferred to eat small children because they were "tender, plump, and rare." Grenier was found insane and locked up in a monastery where he spent his remaining years.

BEAST OR BERSERKER?

In any battle, the person with the most rage often wins. Such was the case with the Viking warriors known as the berserkers. These warriors often wore wolf pelts instead of armor which, according to legend, were magical and put them into a murderous rage with superhuman strength. (*Berserking*, loosely translated from the Old Norse, means going "bear shirt.") Accounts tell of berserkers attacking enemies with their teeth and howling like beasts. It is from the berserkers that we get the term *going berserk*, or "becoming crazy with anger."

One could assume deep-seated rage along with too much Viking high-fiving drove the berserkers to act like beasts, but anthropologists have other ideas. The berserkers may have laced their wine with hallucinogenic drugs to get that ready-for-battle perkiness. Possible suspects are bog myrtle or fly agaric mushrooms. These hallucinogenic drugs can put you into such an altered state that you will act like a crazed wolf. Add the right wolf pelt accessories, and you have all the makings of yet another werewolf legend.

To become more wolflike, the berserkers not only took hallucinogenic drugs and wore animal pelts but also drank the blood of a wolf.

HYPERTRICHOSIS

In 1547, a wolf boy was given as a gift to the queen of France, Catherine de' Medici. He was "not less hairy than a dog," but this boy was no savage monster. His name was Pedro González, and despite looking like a dead ringer for Lon Chaney in *The Wolf Man* (1941), he was just a scared kid stolen from his home in the Canary Islands because he looked different. Pedro was renamed Petrus Gonsalvus, was taught to speak Latin and dress like a nobleman, and was given a position at court. Catherine de' Medici married him to one of her ladies-in-waiting, also named Catherine. Although history does not record many details about their marriage, many scholars believe that Petrus and Catherine's union inspired the original story for *Beauty and the Beast*.

Today we know that Petrus's hairy appearance wasn't because he was a beast. He had an inherited medical condition called **hypertrichosis**, or "werewolf syndrome." Hypertrichosis is caused by a genetic mutation that causes excess hair growth over many parts of the body such as the face and hands. The disease is very rare with fewer than fifty known cases ever recorded.

When Petrus arrived at the French court, people with deformities or even slight abnormalities were believed to be a sign of God's will. They were called *monstrums*, Latin for an unnatural sign of what is to come. It became the origin of the word *monster*.

RABIES

We let our dog lick our face but have a primitive fear of animal bites. This fear of bites comes from the fear of a virus as old as the human race itself: rabies. Rabies is spread from the bite of an infected animal and can turn even a docile lamb into an aggressive, bloodthirsty beast. Before Louis Pasteur discovered the rabies vaccination in 1885, it was 100 percent fatal. It is still nearly 100 percent fatal today if not treated in time. Symptoms of rabies include facial spasms that can make the lips look retracted and the teeth more prominent . . . like a werewolf. It can take three weeks—or several years—for symptoms to appear. When symptoms appear, infected humans often go mad with rage, but they rarely bite.

CANNIBALS & SERIAL KILLERS

During the sixteenth and seventeeth centuries, several people were labeled werewolves after committing some pretty horrific crimes. One of the most famous cases was that of Gilles Garnier, a local hermit who admitted to eating four French children (minus the leg that he saved from one boy). Anyone evil enough to eat children had to be a supernatural monster, not a human. Or so the reasoning went. Unfortunately, people do have the ability to commit heinous crimes without ever leaving their human form. Today, we use the term *serial killer* to describe a person who commits these violent acts repeatedly.

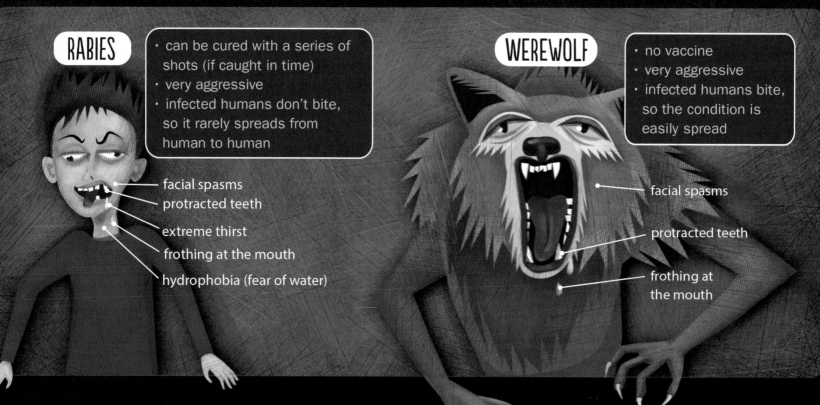

RABIES
- can be cured with a series of shots (if caught in time)
- very aggressive
- infected humans don't bite, so it rarely spreads from human to human

facial spasms
protracted teeth
extreme thirst
frothing at the mouth
hydrophobia (fear of water)

WEREWOLF
- no vaccine
- very aggressive
- infected humans bite, so the condition is easily spread

facial spasms
protracted teeth
frothing at the mouth

HOW TO HOWL LIKE A WEREWOLF

1. Find a high place clear of trees.

2. Take three deep breaths and inhale.

3. Cup your hands around your mouth, and slowly let out an "A-wooooooo" sound.

4. Increase the octave, and then decrease it back down again when you run out of breath.

5. Listen for your pack. If you are in an area with wolves, don't be surprised if you hear a howl back. This is a trick biologists often use to locate wolves.*

*The legal department wants me to remind you that if you howl at a werewolf, it could eat you. Likewise, wolves may try to locate a person if you howl at them. If that happens, remember that although wolves are not likely to attack humans, they are still wild animals and should not be approached.

REAL MONSTERS: SHAPE-SHIFTING BEASTS

You have probably seen chameleons change color depending on their mood, but there are other creatures that can do more than just change color. Much like a werewolf, some creatures can also change shape.

PUNKED-OUT, MUTABLE RAIN FROG

Imagine your face turning from smooth to dragonlike spikes in a matter of seconds. One frog has the ability to do just that. Called the "punk rocker frog," this spiky frog was found by scientists in Ecuador's Andes Mountains. Believing it to be a new species, scientists put it in a plastic cup to be photographed. But the next day, the frog's skin was smooth. Scientists immediately thought they had nabbed the wrong frog and were about to set it free . . . until the frog changed back again.

CROSS-DRESSING CUTTLEFISH

Cuttlefish can not only change their color but can also change the pattern and texture of their skin. Often cuttlefish do this to avoid predators, but sometimes they do it just to fake out their friends. Males will often morph into the muted colors and textures of females on one side while keeping the vibrant colors of males on the other side. They do this to sneak past their male friends, and then once they have found a female . . . they switch to their colorful flashy side and let the flirting begin.

E KRAKEN? THE CLUE IS IN WHALE VOMIT

n the nineteenth century,
ty, gray rock floating along
e known as **ambergris**
ans "gray amber." No one
even what it was, but it
people began using it in
ng. As more and more
me so rare that it was worth
ime hoity-toity aristocrats
e with this strange flotsam,
eally was . . .

In the nineteenth century, thousands of sperm whales were killed for their blubber because it contained precious whale oil used to make soaps and leather, lubricate machinery, and, most important, light lamps throughout the world. When whale hunters in the nineteenth century cut open sperm whales, they found strange beaks inside the whale's stomach coated in the same waxy substance found on beaches—ambergris. They also found 12-inch (30 cm) imprints on the sides of sperm whales as if the whale had been attacked by a Frisbee with hooks. What kind of beaked creature would attack a giant sperm whale? People started to wonder. Could the tales of the kraken be true?

S PERFUME

N. Squid are like milkshakes to
ing a squid doesn't require the
sh any bones because squid are
tes—they lack a spine.

The beak is trapped in intestines and becomes coated with ambergris.

intestines

stomach

2. TRAPPED IN A WHALE. But the
squid's bony beak cannot be digested. It gets trapped and irritates the whale's intestines. The beak is then coated with ambergris in the same way that a oyster will form a pearl around an irritating grain of sand.

MIMIC OCTOPUS

While not exactly shifting from man to beast, the mimic octopus has the ability to transform itself from innocent invertebrate to deadly predator. And unlike werewolves, mimics have more than one shape-shifting trick. Sometimes it will morph into a sea snake or starfish. Other times, its shape-shifting pranks will include poisonous stingrays or jellyfish. Mimic octopuses are such masters of disguise that they will even swim like the sea creatures they are mimicking. Then once their prey has let down their guard, they attack and morph back into their sneaky octopus shape.

The mimic octopus takes on the shape of a poisonous sea snake to scare off predators.

WOLVERINE FROG

Scientists have learned the hard way not to mess with this horror frog. When you pick it up, it appears to have the usual froggy cuteness. But once it is angered, it sprouts razor-sharp, Wolverine-like claws on its rear feet. Called the hairy frog, this creature creates these claws by breaking its bones and shoving them completely through its skin. And just like Wolverine, the frog's claws create tiny wounds, which must later heal. Does it hurt? Only the wolverine frog knows.

Where do you think you are going?

My mistake...

I-AM-BIGGER-THAN-YOU FISH

It is a neat trick when feeling bullied—just shape-shift into something scary. When confronted by predators, a puffer fish can double its size and will sometimes sprout sharp spines to make it look threatening.

If a sea monster larger than a school bus took on a fisherman in a tiny fishing boat, you would probably bet on the sea monster winning. Well, you might want to hold your bets until you meet Theophilus Picot.

On October 25, 1873, Theophilus was fishing off the coast of Newfoundland, Canada, when he spotted what he thought was some debris from a wreck. The fisherman paddled closer to get a better look. A flesh-colored, rounded shape about 60 feet (18 m) long was bobbing up and down in the inky water. Thinking it might be a dead sperm whale, Theophilus poked it with an oar. Bad move. Suddenly, a tentacle shot out of the water with whip-cracking speed. Another tentacle

followed. Eight more ar
like cobras swaying to
lifted a parrotlike bea
dinner plate above t
tentacles wrapped
toothed suction c
pull its prey into
high arc, slicing
turned from pa
sea, leaving a

Now, if T
buddies he
sea monst
drinking to
19-foot (

The
as the
time i
an e
to h
sh
c

86

MIMIC OCTOPUS

While not exactly shifting from man to beast, the mimic octopus has the ability to transform itself from innocent invertebrate to deadly predator. And unlike werewolves, mimics have more than one shape-shifting trick. Sometimes it will morph into a sea snake or starfish. Other times, its shape-shifting pranks will include poisonous stingrays or jellyfish. Mimic octopuses are such masters of disguise that they will even swim like the sea creatures they are mimicking. Then once their prey has let down their guard, they attack and morph back into their sneaky octopus shape.

The mimic octopus takes on the shape of a poisonous sea snake to scare off predators.

WOLVERINE FROG

Scientists have learned the hard way not to mess with this horror frog. When you pick it up, it appears to have the usual froggy cuteness. But once it is angered, it sprouts razor-sharp, Wolverine-like claws on its rear feet. Called the hairy frog, this creature creates these claws by breaking its bones and shoving them completely through its skin. And just like Wolverine, the frog's claws create tiny wounds, which must later heal. Does it hurt? Only the wolverine frog knows.

I-AM-BIGGER-THAN-YOU FISH

It is a neat trick when feeling bullied—just shape-shift into something scary. When confronted by predators, a puffer fish can double its size and will sometimes sprout sharp spines to make it look threatening.

THE KRAKEN

If a sea monster larger than a school bus took on a fisherman in a tiny fishing boat, you would probably bet on the sea monster winning. Well, you might want to hold your bets until you meet Theophilus Picot.

On October 25, 1873, Theophilus was fishing off the coast of Newfoundland, Canada, when he spotted what he thought was some debris from a wreck. The fisherman paddled closer to get a better look. A flesh-colored, rounded shape about 60 feet (18 m) long was bobbing up and down in the inky water. Thinking it might be a dead sperm whale, Theophilus poked it with an oar. Bad move. Suddenly, a tentacle shot out of the water with whip-cracking speed. Another tentacle followed. Eight more arms twisted and undulated in the air like cobras swaying to a snake charmer's flute. The creature lifted a parrotlike beak and an unblinking eye as large as a dinner plate above the surface of the water. One of its long tentacles wrapped around the boat and latched onto it with toothed suction cups. But just as the monster was about to pull its prey into a watery grave, Theophilus swung his ax in a high arc, slicing off the tentacle. The monster's bulbous head turned from pale flesh to bloodred, and it slunk back into the sea, leaving a trail of dark ink in its wake.

Now, if Theophilus had gone home and told his fishing buddies he had freed himself from the death grip of a giant sea monster, they would have probably thought he was drinking too much seawater. But Theophilus had the proof—a 19-foot (6 m) severed tentacle.

The sea monster that attacked Theophilus was known as the kraken (pronounced KRAH-ken), and it wasn't the first time it had terrorized local fishermen. For hundreds of years, an estimated 60-foot (18 m) sea monster was believed to haunt the seas from Norway to Iceland attacking ships, fishermen, whales, and anything else it could wrap its slimy tentacles around.

WHAT IS THE KRAKEN? THE CLUE IS IN WHALE VOMIT

If you were walking along the beach in the nineteenth century, you might have found a fragrant, waxy, gray rock floating along the seashore. This waxy rock became known as **ambergris** (pronounced AM-ber-griz), which means "gray amber." No one knew where ambergris came from or even what it was, but it had such a sweet, earthy scent that people began using it in perfumes, medicine, and even cooking. As more and more people hunted for ambergris, it became so rare that it was worth more than gold. But right about the time hoity-toity aristocrats were flavoring their chocolate mousse with this strange flotsam, people discovered what ambergris really was . . .

In the nineteenth century, thousands of sperm whales were killed for their blubber because it contained precious whale oil used to make soaps and leather, lubricate machinery, and, most important, light lamps throughout the world. When whale hunters in the nineteenth century cut open sperm whales, they found strange beaks inside the whale's stomach coated in the same waxy substance found on beaches—ambergris. They also found 12-inch (30 cm) imprints on the sides of sperm whales as if the whale had been attacked by a Frisbee with hooks. What kind of beaked creature would attack a giant sperm whale? People started to wonder. Could the tales of the kraken be true?

THE KRAKEN BECOMES PERFUME

1. YUMMY KRAKEN. Squid are like milkshakes to sperm whales. Eating a squid doesn't require the whale to crush any bones because squid are invertebrates—they lack a spine.

The beak is trapped in intestines and becomes coated with ambergris.

intestines

stomach

2. TRAPPED IN A WHALE. But the squid's bony beak cannot be digested. It gets trapped and irritates the whale's intestines. The beak is then coated with ambergris in the same way that a oyster will form a pearl around an irritating grain of sand.

HOW TO KEEP A SEA MONSTER IN YOUR BATHTUB

In 1874, shortly after Theophilus Picot's encounter with the sea monster, another sea monster specimen was caught in a fisherman's net nearby and was purchased by the Reverend Moses Harvey. Harvey kept the creature's rotting, 24-foot-long (17 m) body hung over his sponge bath and took great joy in showing his prize off to visitors. (One can assume Harvey didn't take many sponge baths during this period.)

The giant squid in this photo looks pretty big based on the length of its tentacles, but tentacle length can be deceiving. After a squid dies, the tentacles lose their elasticity and will stretch out like the waistband on your favorite sweats. This results in the dead squid being longer than when it was alive.

You smell nice ... like whale vomit.

The giant squid leaves Frisbee-size marks from its tentacles.

4. A FRAGRANT JOURNEY. Ambergris floats in the ocean until it ends up on the shore and is most likely eaten by your dog. In 2012, a UK boy found ambergris worth £40,000 ($55,000).

My tummy hurts.

3. OUT IT COMES. . . . The whale vomits or poops out the indigestible ambergris. When it first comes out, it smells disgusting and is worthless, but over time, it takes on a pleasant, musky smell.

Ambergris is still used in expensive French perfumes to make the scent last, but if you find ambergris along a US beach, you are out of luck. It is illegal to possess ambergris in the US due to the sperm whale's endangered status.

THEORY #1: THE KRAKEN IS A GIANT SQUID

In 1857 Danish naturalist Japetus Steenstrup began compiling data from all the kraken sightings. He believed the kraken wasn't a monster but a kind of squid . . . a monster-sized squid. So, like most faithful scientists of his day, he gave it a proper name—*Architeuthis dux* (pronounced arc-ih-TOOTH-iss DUHKS), otherwise known as the giant squid.

Marine biologists today have identified giant squid as part of the group of ocean invertebrates called **cephalopods**, which includes octopuses, cuttlefish, and nautiluses. *Cephalopod* is Greek for "head foot." That's a strange name to give to a creature that lacks feet. The weirdness doesn't stop there. They have three hearts and their brain wraps around their throat. If you chop off a tentacle, they will bleed tiny drops of blue blood and their tentacle will regenerate. Those tentacles have tiny, sharp teeth on them *and* taste buds. So if you ever find yourself wrapped up in a squid's tentacles, just know that it is not just feeling you out. It is seeing how you taste. And good luck escaping those tentacles. They can whip out in the blink of an eye.

When the dinosaurs died out, squid lived on. There's a reason for that—giant squid are dangerous predators. They can jet backward and forward at 25 miles (40 km) per hour (as fast as sharks). If they catch you, squid experts recommend that you avoid the beak. That is where the real trouble starts.

Squid can also change color to disappear from predators. They even have their own squid arm signal when angered (a raised arm means buzz off dude). When threatened, they shoot blue-black ink out of a special sac connected to their anus and pumped through a funnel. Yes, that's right. They shoot ink out of their butts to confuse predators. Like a magician disappearing in a cloud of smoke, the squid takes off and the whale is left attacking their ink fart.

With an average length of around 33 feet (10 m) combined with their freakish appearance, you can see why the giant squid has long been thought to be the source of the kraken legend. But then scientists found an even scarier monster . . .

WHY GIANT SQUID ARE NOT ON THE MENU

The giant squid's pockets in its muscles are filled with ammonia. Since ammonia is less dense than seawater, it allows the squid to float along without much effort. Those pockets of ammonia also make the squid taste and smell like urine mixed with cleaning fluid (at least to humans). Squid expert Clyde Roper once served up giant squid to his guests. He said it tasted just like it smelled—"bitter."

I wish we tasted like wet diapers.

Yeah, then we would not get eaten.

GIANT SQUID ARE REALLY WEIRD
...EVEN WEIRDER THAN THE KRAKEN

LIMBS WITH TASTE BUDS
Their tentacles have suckers and taste buds.

GONADS
Males inject sperm into the female's arm to mate.

FIN

GIANT EYES Eyes are roughly 10.6 inches (27 cm), about the size of a dinner plate.

SYSTEMIC HEART

STOMACH

SMELLS LIKE PEE
Their muscles are filled with ammonia that makes them smell and taste like urine.

MANTLE

ARM SIGNALS
A raised arm means back off.

BRAIN WRAPS AROUND THE THROAT

COMMUNICATE WITH LIGHT
They use chromatophores—light-reflecting skin cells that change colors and flash patterns.

GILL HEART
They have one on each side.

INK SAC
It stores ink.

GILLS

SHOOT INK OUT OF BUTT
To confuse predators, it shoots ink out of its funnel.

SHARP BIRDLIKE BEAK
To eat you. The beak is about the size of your hand.

TONGUE WITH ROWS OF TEETH
To grind up your body. A squid's tongue is called a radula.

BLEED BLUE
They bleed blue because of the copper in their blood.

CHOPPED-OFF ARMS THAT KEEP MOVING
A severed arm can continue to grab for several hours afterwards.

Stay away from the beak!

THEORY #2: THE KRAKEN IS A COLOSSAL SQUID

The first colossal squid (*Mesonychoteuthis hamiltoni*) was found in 1925 when a fisherman removed it from the stomach of a sperm whale. Six out of the eight colossal squid since then were found in sperm whales. In 2007, a fishing boat caught a 1,091-pound (495 kg) colossal squid in the Ross Sea, Antarctica. The squid was frozen and gifted to researchers at the Te Papa museum in New Zealand so they could study its anatomy.

The colossal squid is not a creature to mess with. Instead of having razor-sharp teeth on its tentacles like its cousin the giant squid has, the colossal squid has rotating hooks to grasp onto prey in the ultimate death grip.

But despite being a dangerous predator, the colossal squid is unlikely to have been the source of Scandinavian kraken legends because it is typically found in the Southern Hemisphere near Antarctica. It also is not known to attack humans (so far).

SIZE COMPARISON (ESTIMATED AVERAGES)

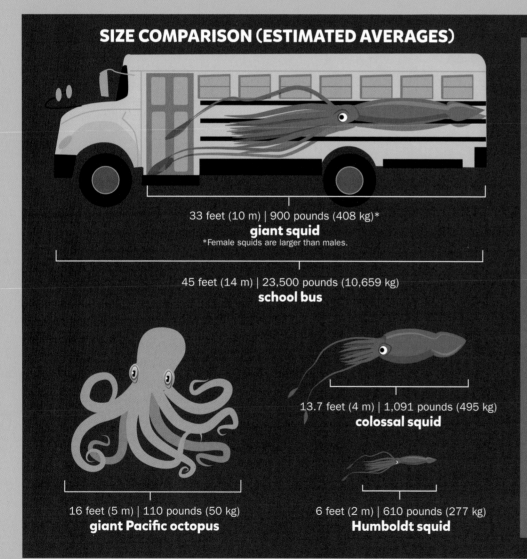

33 feet (10 m) | 900 pounds (408 kg)*
giant squid
*Female squids are larger than males.

45 feet (14 m) | 23,500 pounds (10,659 kg)
school bus

16 feet (5 m) | 110 pounds (50 kg)
giant Pacific octopus

13.7 feet (4 m) | 1,091 pounds (495 kg)
colossal squid

6 feet (2 m) | 610 pounds (277 kg)
Humboldt squid

HOW DOES THE KRAKEN SEE?

The colossal squid has the largest eyes of any creature—as big as soccer balls. Like your eyes, the colossal uses **binocular vision**—their eyes face forward to see objects in the distance (like an approaching sperm whale).

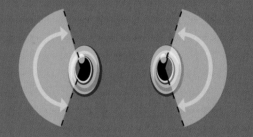

The giant squid's eyes are about the size of dinner plates. Like most fish and birds, giant squid and octopuses have monocular vision—their eyes are on the sides of their head. This allows it to see better forward and behind it, but not at longer distances.

THEORY #3: THE KRAKEN IS A HUMBOLDT SQUID

Squid expert Clyde Roper has argued that giant and colossal squid never come to the surface of the water unless they are injured or dying. But all the kraken encounters of the last two centuries seem to tell tales of feisty beasts not ready to kick the bucket. Sailors in the nineteenth century claimed the kraken would even jump out of the water and attack ships.

There is one species of squid vicious enough to attack humans—the Humboldt squid (*Dosidicus gigas*). Humboldt squid only reach about 6 feet (1.8 m) in total length, but some marine biologists have wondered if there may be gigantic Humboldts lurking in the deepest levels of the ocean. Normally, Humboldts are found at depths of 2,000 feet (610 m), but they will rise to the surface when hungry. And because they grow 3 feet (0.9 m) in a single year, they are always hungry. Humboldt squid have been spotted leaping out of the water at such high speeds that they appear to be flying.

If attacked by one, be prepared for a bite force equal to an African lion's—enough to cut through solid bone. Mexican fishermen claim that if you fall into a pack of them, by the time you reach the ocean floor, only your skeleton will remain.

Found mostly off the coast of California, Mexico, and South America, the Humboldt is known as the "red devil" because it turns red to camouflage itself. Turning red hides the Humboldt because deep-sea creatures cannot see the color red. (Red light does not penetrate that deep.) Could tales of the kraken be describing this squid?

THEORY #4: THE KRAKEN IS A GIANT OCTOPUS

In 2011 paleontologist Mark McMenamin found an odd arrangement of fossilized bones in a state park in Nevada. The bones belonged to the ichthyosaur, a prehistoric sea reptile that lived during the Triassic period. The ichthyosaur resembled a dolphin with a potbelly, except MUCH larger—45 feet (14 m) long. A bottlenose dolphin averages 8 feet (2.4 m) in length.

The fossilized bones were found in a lair with markings similar to how Humboldt squid attack their prey, but with one difference—the bones were arranged in a pattern that looked like abstract art. McMenamin theorized that a large cephalopod killed the ichthyosaur and then played with its food.

At first, the scientific community was doubtful of the findings. Where were the cephalopod's fossil remains? Unfortunately, finding a cephalopod fossil is tricky because it doesn't have hard bits like bones that can become fossils. But cephalopods can leave behind their very hard beaks.

Two years later, McMenamin found a fossilized beak on the same site where he found the bone art. This meant that the ichthyosaur and the mystery predator did meet. But what kind of beaked creature could not only take down an ichthyosaur but also be clever enough to make art with its bones?

While scientists are still figuring out how intelligent squid are, one beaked creature they know to be highly intelligent is the octopus. In laboratory tests, octopuses can open childproof jars and solve mazes. (Squid can't master these tricks yet.) In several laboratories, octopuses have been known to escape their aquarium through small crevices. Sometimes they sneak into neighboring aquariums during the night where they feast on smaller study subjects and then return to their aquarium by morning to avoid blame.

Octopuses are also known for taking apart objects and tinkering with them. In one New Zealand aquarium, trainers taught an octopus to snap pictures of gawking visitors by using an underwater camera. (The octopus has yet to master selfies.)

Lastly, octopuses are certainly mischievous enough to play with their food. They will often bring bones back to their dens and arrange them in a pattern. Octopuses love home decorating.

The largest octopus ever found was a giant Pacific octopus measuring 30 feet (9 m) across and weighing over 600 pounds (272 kg). Could the kraken really be a a giant octopus?

HOME
SWEET
HOME

HOW TO TELL IF YOU ARE ABOUT TO BE EATEN
BY A GIANT OCTOPUS

RAISES ITS MANTLE
It will raise the bulbous part of its head called a mantle above its eyes.

GETS LARGE . . .
An angry octopus will spread itself out and lengthen to its full height.

OR SMALL
When threatened, a hungry octopus can squeeze into any shape bigger than its eyeball, so you have nowhere to hide.

INJECTS POISON
All octopuses inject venom into their prey. The blue-ringed octopus' venom will kill a human in minutes.

IF YOU MUST WRESTLE AN OCTOPUS . . .
In the 1960s, octopus wrestling became a popular sport. Divers would jump into frigid waters to wrestle an octopus out of the water. Whoever captured the largest octopus won. This angered a lot of octopuses. Octopus wrestling has since become illegal unless you plan to eat it.

CHANGES COLOR
A mad octopus will turn darker and form bumps along its skin. A relaxed octopus will be paler.

SQUIRTS WATER
A mad octopus will shoot water out of its funnel at an annoying person. They also do this while playing in the same way you might use a squirt gun.

THEY GET VENGEFUL
Octopuses are intelligent enough to hold a grudge, and they recognize people by sight. If you anger one, don't expect this monster to forget.

TIP: Most octopuses will not attack humans, but they have been known to attack other dangerous predators like sharks and fellow octopuses. If the kraken is an octopus, then it is best to know when you have angered one so you can try to escape.

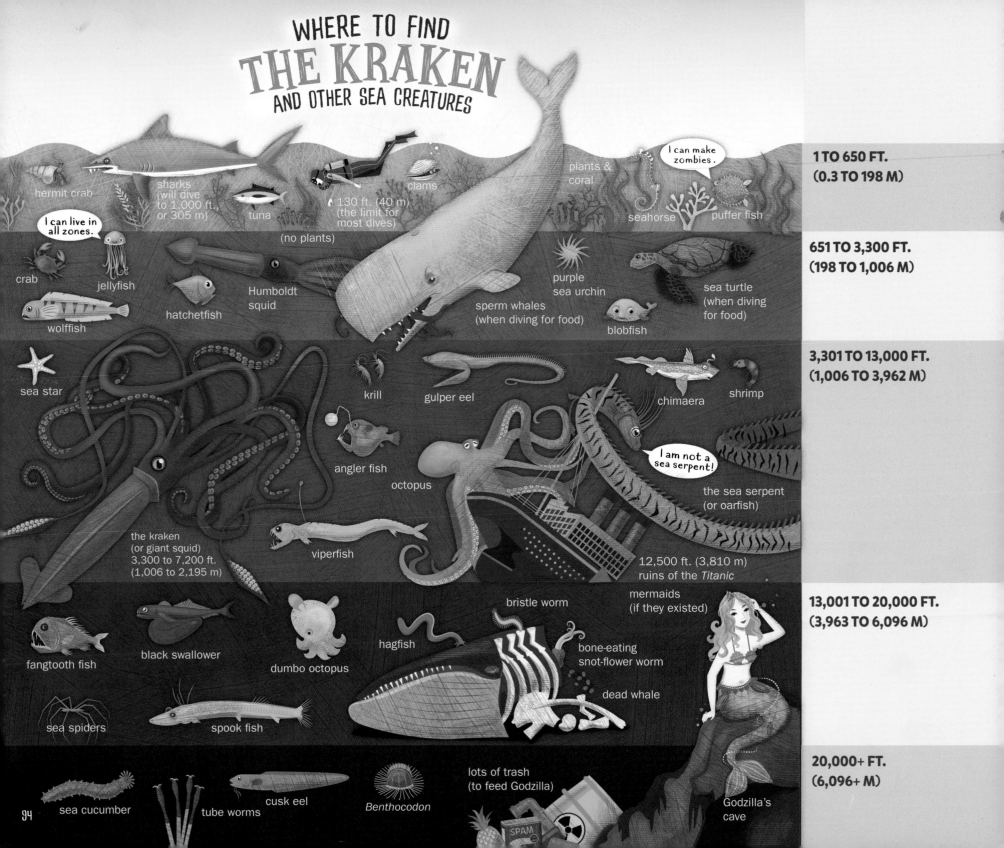

THE ZONES

The ocean is divided into five main layers called zones. By understanding the characteristics and sea creatures living in each zone, we have a better chance of finding the kraken.

All the yummy snacks are in this zone.

SUNLIGHT ZONE

This is where **photosynthesis** occurs—the process by which plants use light to make food. This zone is brimming with an array of sea life, making it great if you are large and looking for lots of menu choices and bad if you are on the menu.

TWILIGHT ZONE

This zone is too dark for photosynthesis, so no plant life grows here. Because the sunlight zone is the most dangerous for prey, many sea creatures stay in the twilight zone by day and go up to the sunlight zone at night. With less light, this zone is also a lot colder (39°F to 41°F, 4°C to 5°C).

MIDNIGHT ZONE

No sunlight penetrates this zone, and temperatures are much colder (39°F, or 4°C). Because red light cannot be detected, red creatures like the colossal squid and kraken appear as black as the water and can easily hide. Food is also scarce. To conserve energy, many predators camouflage themselves and then attack unsuspecting prey. Others, like the anglerfish, use a glowing light to lure prey to their sharp teeth. This ability to produce light is called **bioluminescence**. Some marine life use bioluminescence to hide, while others use it to signal to other marine life. Two-thirds of all squid are bioluminescent, so most likely the kraken has its own light show too.

Pretty light.

ABYSSAL ZONE

Things are getting strange in the abyssal zone. Fish like the spook fish have eyes that point upward to spot predators above them, while the fangtooth fish sport the largest teeth in relation to their body of any fish. You will also find whale carcasses on the ocean floor with hagfish feeding on their blubber and muscle while the bristle worm and bone-eating snot-flower worm feed on their bones. It can take one hundred years for the entire whale to be eaten.

DEEPSEA CHALLENGER

In 2012, James Cameron, filmmaker and director of the blockbuster movie *Titanic*, made a record-breaking dive to the Mariana Trench. The vertical shape of the sub, named the Deepsea Challenger, allowed Cameron to reach the bottom quicker and spend more time on the ocean floor.

35,756 ft. (10,898 m)

TRENCH ZONE

With water temperatures barely above freezing, high pressures, and depths up to 7 miles (11 km) below the surface, scientists believe this zone is sparsely populated.

THE KRAKEN VS. SCIENCE: WHO WOULD WIN?

In many kraken tales, the monster is strong enough to pull a ship to the bottom of the sea. But could a sea monster really have the strength to pull a ship underwater?

To answer that question, think of what happens when you put a rock and a beach ball in your tub. The rock will sink and the beach ball will float, right? This is not due to their weight but their density.

THE KRAKEN VS. DENSITY

Both a rock and a beach ball are made of molecules—tiny atoms bonded together. If you looked deep inside the rock and the beach ball with a microscope, you would find the rock's molecules packed tightly together but the air-filled beach ball's molecules spread farther apart. How closely molecules are held together in a space is called density. The closer molecules are packed together, the denser the object is. Objects that are denser than the surrounding water sink. This is also one of the reasons why heavy ships can float. The bottom part of the ship, called the hull, is an empty space filled with air.

THE KRAKEN VS. BUOYANT FORCE

Now think of the last time you tried to pull a beach ball underwater. When you throw a beach ball in the water, gravity is pushing down on it, but as soon as it hits the water, the water pushes back. When you then try to pull the beach ball underwater, the water below the beach ball pushes underneath it, and you must fight that force. The water level then rises and pushes a beach ball-sized amount of water out of the way. The upward force from the water on the ball is called buoyant force. The buoyant force wins (usually), and as you try to pull the beach ball down, it bounces out of the water, smacking you in the face. If the kraken tried to pull a ship underwater, it might not get smacked in the face with the ship, but it would have a hard time pulling it under due to the buoyant force on the ship.

As gravity and the kraken push down on the ball, the water pushes back. This is called buoyant force. When objects float, the buoyant force is equal to the weight of the water pushed out of the way.

gravity

The rock sinks because its molecules are packed tightly together, making it denser than the water.

molecules

The beach ball floats because its molecules are spread farther apart, making it less dense than the water.

Curse you, buoyant force!

buoyant force

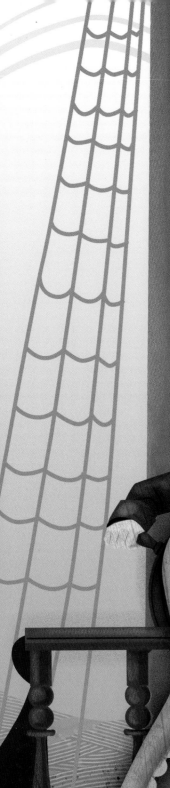

If the kraken is a giant squid, there is another reason why it would have a hard time pulling a ship underwater. A beach ball floats because it is filled with air, which is less dense than the surrounding water. Similarily, a giant squid's muscles are filled with ammonia, which is also less dense than the surrounding water (p. 88). Therefore, to pull a ship underwater, a giant squid must overcome its own buoyancy. This would be similar to you pulling a person underwater while wearing a life jacket. Not easy!

Science always wins over the kraken . . .

Sperm whales are not usually aggressive. Whale experts believe many whale attacks throughout history were caused by whales accidentally bumping into ships.

SEA MONSTERS WHO DO SINK SHIPS

One way a kraken could pull a ship underwater is if it smashed it into pieces. Neither giant squid nor octopus are known to use their tentacles or mantle like a sledgehammer, but there is one creature who batters ships—sperm whales.

Sperm whales have every right to want to smash ships. By 1853, eight thousand whales were being slaughtered a year. During this time, one particularly vengeful albino whale attacked over one hundred ships but always seemed to escape the sharp harpoons of whalers. Sailors named this particularly vicious whale Mocha Dick because it was sighted off the coast of Chile near Mocha Island (and perhaps because Mocha Richard is not a strong enough pet name for a vengeful whale). But Mocha Dick was not just a sailor's tall tale. Recently, scientists found a graveyard of sunken whale ships thousands of meters below the calm surface of the water where Mocha Dick would attack.

In 1852, author Herman Melville drew inspiration from his time spent on a whaling ship and stories of these whale attacks to write a novel about a hateful whale. Melville named his whale Moby Dick.

Ouch. You bumped my head.

HOW TO CATCH A KRAKEN

On September 30, 2004, zoologists from the National Museum of Nature and Science in Japan were the first to capture a giant squid on camera. Then in 2013, after fifty-five dives into the ocean depths, a team of researchers took the first live video of a giant squid. If you would rather catch a giant squid (or something larger) instead of some tiny, boring fish on your next fishing trip, here is how to do it:

1. CHOOSE THE RIGHT SPOT. The crew chose the Ogasawara Islands in the North Pacific Ocean because sperm whale can be found there. Sperm whale eat giant squid, so where there are sperm whales, there are giant squid.

2. GO DEEP. Giant squid are found where no light penetrates the ocean, so you are going to have to use a long fishing line. The scientists lowered their bait and camera with a light attached to it 3,000 feet (914 m) deep (about a half a mile).

Japan

Ogasawara Islands

3. USE THE RIGHT BAIT. The researchers attached common squid and chopped-up shrimp to two hooks. Giant squid eat other squid.

4. BE PREPARED FOR A STRUGGLE. While catching a trout or two can be pretty simple, reeling in a sea monster is going to take some muscle. Giant squid were once believed to be ambush hunters. Ambush hunters hang out on the ocean floor and wait for their prey to come to them. But recent footage of the giant squid shows a very active predator. In the 2004 expedition, the giant squid attacked the lure and was so determined to break free that it severed its own tentacle. The zoologists were left with only an 18-foot (5.5 m), sticky tentacle on their hook . . . that was still moving. The dismembered limb even continued to grab members of the team with its toothed suckers.

5. DON'T TURN ON THE LIGHTS. It can be tricky to sneak up on a creature that has eyes as big as a dinner plate. Those big eyes help the giant squid see in front and behind it, so researchers used a camera called the Medusa, which emitted only red light. Giant squid cannot see red light, so the camera did not scare it off.

6. BE VERY QUIET. Sound travels farther than light in the deep ocean, so the kraken may hear us before it can see us. Researchers suspected the electrical thrusters, which powered the submersible cameras, might be scaring off the giant squid. The solution was to use a quieter, battery-operated camera.

7. FAKE IT OUT. The team used a lure that mimicked the same light display made by an Atolla jellyfish. Squid are attracted to jellyfish, not because they want to eat them (they are too small to provide much of a meal) but because jellyfish emit a flashing light when a larger predator attacks them. This flashing device acted like a dinner bell and tricked the squid into thinking a jellyfish was under attack by a larger predator, which would provide a much bigger meal.

8. WEAR BLACK. If you do catch a giant squid, its first instinct will be to spray you with blue-black ink. You might want to save your light-colored clothes for other fishing trips.

SNEAKING UP ON A KRAKEN
A team of researchers used the following device to sneak up on a giant squid.

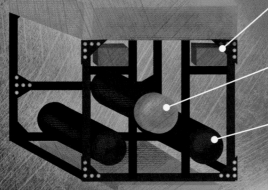

FAR-RED LED ILLUMINATORS
The giant squid cannot see red light, so it does not get scared away.

CAMERA
It is used to capture a picture of a giant squid or other sea monster.

BATTERY-POWERED MOTOR
A quiet, battery-powered motor is used so as not to scare the giant squid.

E-JELLY
The giant squid is attracted to the light because it mimics a jellyfish's flashing lights.

Pretty light...

REAL MONSTERS: DEEP-SEA GIGANTISM

The kraken is not the only sea creature that has grown into an enormous monster. Over the last roughly five hundred million years, the size of some deep-sea marine life has grown 150 times larger. When deep sea animals get larger than their shallow-water cousins, it is called deep-sea gigantism. Scientists are not 100 percent sure what causes deep-sea gigantism. One hypothesis is that there are fewer predators at deeper sea levels. With few predators, there are less chances of getting killed, so your typical crab can get fat and happy instead of ending up on the dinner plate. Another hypothesis is that animals in colder temperatures have slower metabolisms and, consequently, need less food.

Unfortunately, ocean temperatures are heating up now due to global warming, and this has many marine biologists worried. If ocean waters get warmer, then it will make sea monsters hungrier and force them to shallower waters for a snack. And isn't a giant sea spider invading your vacation spot reason enough to control global warming?

30.5 feet (9.3 m)

THE REAL SEA SERPENT

In 2013 two oarfish washed up on California beaches, causing the public to speculate that sea serpents might be invading the coast. With its silvery, sinuous body and dragonlike red crest, the oarfish is one of the most fantastical-looking giants of the deep sea. They are the largest bony fish in existence but are rarely seen at shallow depths unless they are injured or dying.

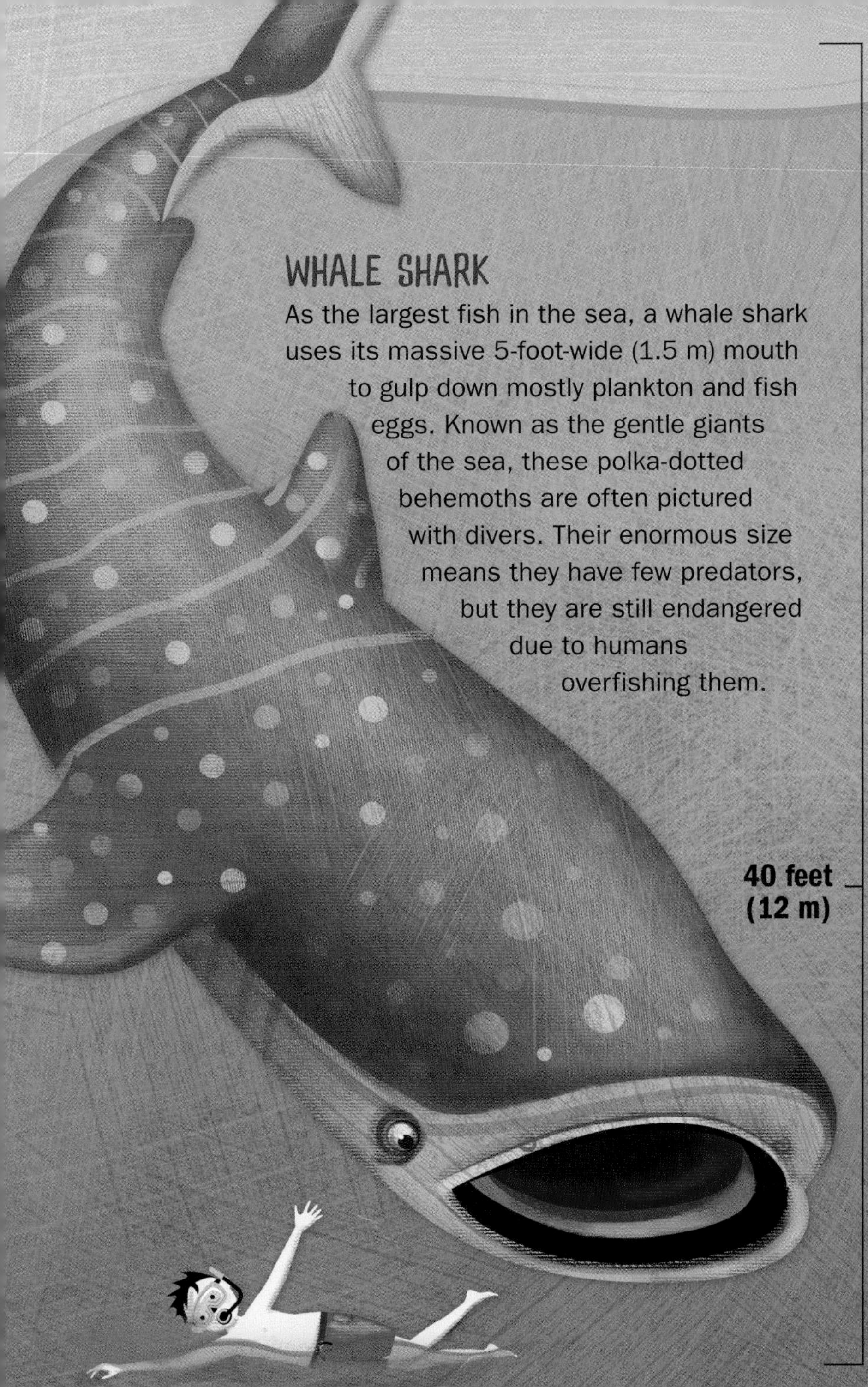

WHALE SHARK

As the largest fish in the sea, a whale shark uses its massive 5-foot-wide (1.5 m) mouth to gulp down mostly plankton and fish eggs. Known as the gentle giants of the sea, these polka-dotted behemoths are often pictured with divers. Their enormous size means they have few predators, but they are still endangered due to humans overfishing them.

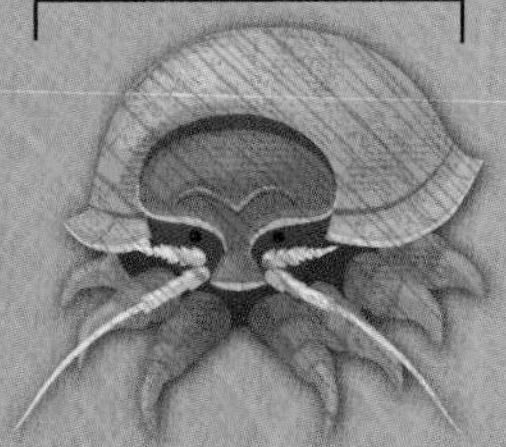

40 feet
(12 m)

SIZE COMPARISON

7.5 to 14 inches
(19 to 36 cm)

GIANT ISOPOD

Some people find them adorable (as if a giant roach-like creature that feeds on rotting fish flesh could be cute). Their glowing eyes and four sets of jaws certainly give them the appearance of a nightmarish insect, but they are actually crustaceans—the same family as crabs and shrimp. Isopods usually are between 3 and 6 inches (7.6 to 15 cm), but giant ones can reach up to 30 inches (76 cm)—the size of a small dog. And like their relative the pill bug, they roll up into a ball when threatened. Maybe then they look cute.

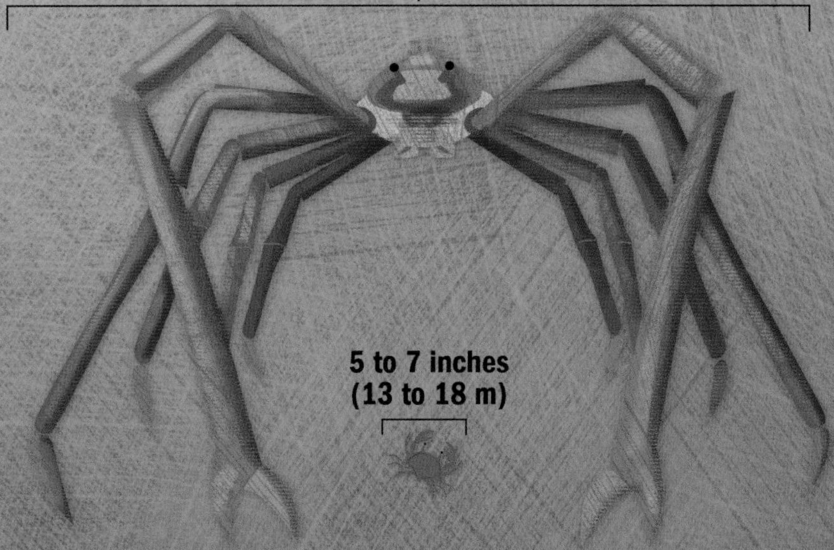

13 feet, or 4 m (from claw to claw)

5 to 7 inches
(13 to 18 m)

CRABZILLA

Afraid of spiders? Have no fear. The Japanese spider crab isn't really a spider (it's a crab), nor is it interested in biting your toes. It will pretty much eat anything but prefers to scavenge for dead things and was once rumored to feed on the bodies of drowned sailors. Today researchers have found they are quite gentle, even though their claws can crush a coconut in half.

BIGFOOT

"Look at these tracks . . ."

In 2013 eleven-year-old Yevgeny Anisimov was playing with his two friends when he stumbled upon strange tracks on a snow-covered field in the Kemerovo region of Siberia. The footprints looked like a human's footprint except for one thing. They were gigantic—16 inches (41 cm) long and 6 to 8 inches (15 to 20 cm) wide. The unusual size was not all that caught his attention. The feet made an odd trail in the snow. Not side by side like a human's prints, but toe to heel, as if the owner had walked across an invisible tightrope.

The excited boys followed the winding trail of footprints until it ended at a heavily wooded forest. Then they saw it. Through a few fallen trees, a dark brown, hairy monster glared at the three boys. His eyes were like a human's eyes, but his arms were unnaturally long and his lower jaw protruded like that of an ape. But what most terrified the boys was that he was big . . . really big.

At that point, one of the boys remembered thinking, "I am going to be eaten!" But instead, the creature dashed off. Not on all fours like a startled animal, but on two legs, as graceful as a ballet dancer exiting stage right.

Now, if the boys had returned home and told their parents they had seen a big, hairy monster, no one would have believed them. But the boys had a shocking piece of evidence that made their story credible: Yevgeny Anisimov had recorded the entire encounter on his iPhone.

Since that recording, forensic researchers in Cambridge, UK, have examined his video to determine if it is fake. The result? The video was never doctored. Skeptics say the monster in the boy's video is just a bear or perhaps a tall man dressed in a hair suit. But to this day, Yevgeny swears that the video is not a hoax and is still too terrified to return to the location where he saw the monster.

Several people who have seen the video have claimed the monster is the legendary Bigfoot, otherwise known as Sasquatch, yeti, yowie, or the skunk ape. The descriptions vary, but people often describe Bigfoot as apelike, with dark brown, black, reddish, or white hair, and usually bipedal—walking on two legs. Many eyewitnesses report a distinctive musty odor around the creature described as a cross between putrid cabbage, rotting eggs, and dead skunk. Bigfoot believers claim the beast often knocks on wood or throws rocks to scare off hunters. They also say you can tell if a Bigfoot lives in an area because it leaves behind a triangular-shaped nest made from branches and tree bark. But the telltale sign that an area is "squatchy" is always some seriously large footprints.

THE FIRST BIG BIGFOOT FOOTPRINTS

In 1958 Jerry Crew and his construction team were building a road in Bluff Creek, California, when they saw something strange—giant footprints stamped into the mud along Trinity River. Then more odd things started happening in Bluff Creek: a 450-pound (204 kg) drum of diesel fuel (far too heavy to be lifted by men) was thrown into the creek, dogs went missing, and more and more large footprints were found in the dust. Crew made a plaster cast of one those footprints and took it to the local newspaper. The press ran with the story, and the mysterious beast that terrorized Bluff Creek was given a name: Bigfoot.

Over the years, people continued to speculate about whether Bigfoot was real or imaginary. Then, in 2002,

newspapers reported a very different headline—"Bigfoot is dead." He died because a man named Ray Wallace also died and his family came forward with an intriguing tale. Wallace claimed he had tricked Jerry Crew in 1958 by strapping large, wooden feet to his legs and stomping all over the construction site at Bluff Creek. It would appear the case was closed except for one odd detail. The crude wooden feet the family claimed Wallace had used in his prank did not match the plaster cast made by Jerry Crew of the footprints. But Wallace's wooden feet did match other plaster casts of footprints made at the site. Is it possible that some tracks were fake, while others were real?

1800s
Pacific Northwest Native American tribes report seeing "wild men."

1782
Pioneer Daniel Boone claims to have shot a large hairy beast called a "Yahoo."

1893
In his book *The Wilderness Hunter*, future president Theodore Roosevelt writes of an encounter with a large, hairy monster that attacks and kills a hunter.

BIGFOOT'S FILM DEBUT

Seeing big footprints is one thing, but seeing an actual Bigfoot is quite another. In 1967 an ex-rodeo cowboy named Roger Patterson claimed he did just that. In the same area as Crew's footprints, he filmed a Bigfoot on his 16 mm handheld Kodak movie camera. In the grainy, jumpy, 59.5-second clip, what is believed to be a female Bigfoot casually walks across a sandy dune strewn with broken branches. All the typical Bigfoot features are there: hairy ape body, slightly pointed head, and humanlike face. At one point, she turns and fixates a haunting glare at the camera as if to say, "I am allowing you to look at me."

The video clip has been picked apart for the last fifty years with no one being able to determine what the creature dubbed "Patty" really is. Is she an ape? Is she a man in an ape suit? Primate experts point out that she has some very un-apelike features. Apes cannot turn their heads the way she does. Apes also do not have hair on their breasts, and Patty clearly does.

If Patty is a man in an ape suit, no one can make the arm and leg proportions match a man's proportions. Patty has long upper legs and short lower legs that would be highly unlikely in a human. Since the Patterson video, a few hypotheses have been developed on what Bigfoot might be . . .

BIGFOOT CROSSING

PRESENT
Over three thousand Bigfoot sightings are reported every year throughout the US.

1995
The Bigfoot Field Researchers Organization is established to track all Bigfoot sightings.

1958
Jerry Crew makes a plaster cast of large footprints found at Bluff Creek, California. The monster is given a name: Bigfoot.

2002
Ray Wallace dies, and his family claims the footprints at Bluff Creek were made with wooden feet.

1967
Roger Patterson records video of a female Bigfoot in Bluff Creek, California.

WHAT IS BIGFOOT? CAN YOU SOLVE THE MYSTERY?

THEORY 1:
BIGFOOT IS HUMAN . . . EXCEPT SMARTER

Igor Burtsev, who heads the Moscow-based International Center of Hominology, thinks he knows why we can't find solid evidence of Bigfoot. Bigfoot is just too smart. According to Burtsev, Bigfoot may have superior intelligence because he may be our closest extinct relative, *Homo neanderthalensis*, otherwise known as a Neanderthal (pronounced nee-AN-der-tall). About forty-five thousand years ago, *Homo sapiens* (a.k.a. humans) moved out of Africa into Europe and Asia. That's when they met Neanderthals. We don't really know what went down next. It could have been fisticuffs. (Fossil evidence shows *Homo*

The Neanderthal Next Door
Neanderthals didn't really look like the hairy, menacing Bigfoot haunting the forests of the Pacific Northwest. Most Neanderthals had light hair, light skin, elongated skulls, and averaged about 5 feet 5 inches (1.7 m). Most likely, if a Neanderthal was walking down the street today, you would think he was just a short, blond-haired guy with a football-shaped skull and some questionable fashion sense. If Neanderthals evolved into today's Bigfoot, they would have gone through adaptation—the changes that make a species better suited to its environment. For example, scientists believe Neanderthals adapted to have a shorter, stockier build because it helped them survive colder climates.

sapiens might have eaten Neanderthals.) Or it could have been a fast friendship. (DNA evidence shows Neanderthals liked *Homo sapiens* enough to have kids with them.) What we do know is we survived, and Neanderthals did not.

Scientists today still do not know why Neanderthals went extinct. We ate similar foods, wore similar things, used similar tools, and both cooked with fire. Some scientists like Burtsev have wondered if they simply got tired of the *Homo sapiens* hogging all the woolly mammoths and decided to hide in the forests, swamps, and mountainous regions. In other words, what if Neanderthals didn't completely die off and instead became Bigfoot? Perhaps Bigfoot is reading this book right now in his comfy stick shelter and laughing his big, hairy butt off at our stupidity.

> Hey! My butt is not this big! Just my feet are . . .

THE EVOLUTION OF BIGFOOT

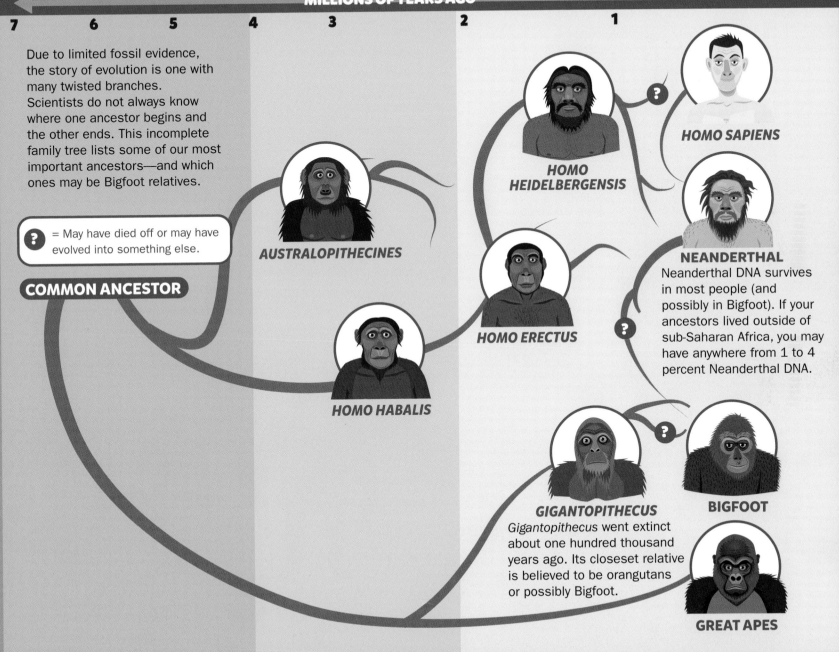

MILLIONS OF YEARS AGO

7 6 5 4 3 2 1

Due to limited fossil evidence, the story of evolution is one with many twisted branches. Scientists do not always know where one ancestor begins and the other ends. This incomplete family tree lists some of our most important ancestors—and which ones may be Bigfoot relatives.

? = May have died off or may have evolved into something else.

COMMON ANCESTOR

AUSTRALOPITHECINES

HOMO HABALIS

HOMO ERECTUS

HOMO HEIDELBERGENSIS

HOMO SAPIENS

NEANDERTHAL
Neanderthal DNA survives in most people (and possibly in Bigfoot). If your ancestors lived outside of sub-Saharan Africa, you may have anywhere from 1 to 4 percent Neanderthal DNA.

GIGANTOPITHECUS
Gigantopithecus went extinct about one hundred thousand years ago. Its closeset relative is believed to be orangutans or possibly Bigfoot.

BIGFOOT

GREAT APES

THEORY 2:
BIGFOOT IS AN APE

In 1935 anthropologist Gustav Heinrich Ralph von Koenigswald discovered "dragon's teeth" were being ground up as a pain medicine in an apothecary shop in Liuzhou, China. They were three times the size of human molars and really weren't doing a thing for anyone's back pain. Von Koenigswald recognized that the teeth were not from dragons but from extinct apes that lived over three hundred thousand years ago. He named this ape *Gigantopithecus blacki*—Latin for "gigantic ape." It is believed that *Gigantopithecus* (Giganto) was about 10 feet (3 m) tall and weighed about 500 pounds (227 kg)—the largest ape ever recorded. Its closest living relative is the orangutan, and it was the only ape to go extinct in the Pleistocene age.

human vs. Giganto molar

Skeptics have questioned that if Bigfoot once lived in North America, why hasn't anyone found any fossil remains similar to those of Giganto? To date, no great ape fossils have been found in North America. But fossil creation is rare, and many species die out without ever leaving a fossil record behind. The question remains puzzling, but without a fossil, the theory that Bigfoot is an ape remains unproven.

A. HERBIVORE
It ate mostly plants.

B. APPEARANCE?
Because only the jaw and teeth have been found, it is impossible to know what Giganto looked like.

C. LARGE SIZE
10 feet (3 m) tall
500 pounds (227 kg)

C. BIPEDAL?
Most likely a knuckle walker, similar to gorillas, but it could have stood upright.

IS BIGFOOT GIGANTO?
Some cryptologists have claimed that *Gigantopithecus blacki* is the legendary primate known as Bigfoot, Yeren, or yeti.

GIGANTOPITHECUS BLACKI
Miocene-Pleistocene
(Six million to two hundred thousand years ago)

GIGANTOPITHECUS
10 feet tall (3 m)
500 pounds (277 kg)

BIGFOOT
6 to 10 feet tall
(1.8 to 3 m)
400 to 1,000 pounds
(181 to 454 kg)

HUMAN
5 feet 10 inches
(1.8 m)
198 pounds (89 kg)

THEORY #3:
SQUATCHY OR BLOTCHY?

In most of the videos and photos taken by witnesses, Bigfoot often looks like a blurry or grainy blob. Thus, the term *blobsquatch* was coined by skeptics tired of Bigfoot believers claiming every rock, tree, wild animal, or thumbprint on their photo was Bigfoot. These skeptics continue to argue that if Bigfoot is really wandering around in the forest, then why in this age of advanced cell phone cameras and hovering drones is our best evidence a grainy old video from the 1960s? And why can't anyone get a single piece of hair off Bigfoot's head? Or how about some Bigfoot scat (a.k.a. poop)? Surely, he must poop. Physical remains such as hair and poop are important because they would contain Bigfoot's DNA—the genetic blueprint that would tell scientists if Bigfoot is an ape, human, or alien. But first, we have to find physical evidence.

That's how the zoological world works. **Cryptids** are just fairy tales and mythical creatures until they are identified as a species—a group of organisms capable of producing fertile offspring. Currently, Bigfoot is not a species. He is just a shadowy figure sometimes caught on blurry video recordings. But with a little DNA or a legitimate fossil, Bigfoot could easily go from being a monster myth to a classified species of bear, ape, or even hominin.

APPLYING SCIENCE TO BIGFOOT

In 2014 Bryan Sykes, professor of human genetics at Oxford University, put out a call to all Bigfoot hunters—show me the hair. After collecting hair samples from around the world, he ran DNA analysis on thirty of them. Unfortunately, the results were disappointing for Bigfoot believers. The hair showed black bear, polar bear, white-tailed deer, canine (wolf or dog), horse, raccoon, and porcupine matches. But no Bigfoot.

WHY BIGFOOT LOOKS LIKE AN APE (AND YOU DON'T)

Many sightings of Bigfoot describe a hairy, apelike creature that looks human, except for the protruding mouth. It is one of the mysteries of Bigfoot. Why does his face resemble an ape more than a human? The answer to that question may be in how we evolved and he did not.

The human race's evolutionary past was pretty violent. Our cavedwelling ancestors did not shoot one another or explode bombs, but we did punch one another in the face a lot. We punched one another enough times that some scientists believe our skulls evolved to withstand those punches.

In particular, our ancestors' jawbones and cheekbones became larger and broader, while the bones across the nose and eyes became thicker. Eventually, humans ended up with noses and jaws less likely to break.

HANDS EVOLVED FOR KNUCKLE SANDWICHES
Some scientists believe our once-apelike hands also evolved for combat. Unlike apes (or Bigfoot), we can form a fist with the thumb outside the fingers. When apes fight, their thumbs are too short to form fists. Instead, they wrestle, hold their

HOW OUR SKULLS EVOLVED TO GET PUNCHED IN THE FACE

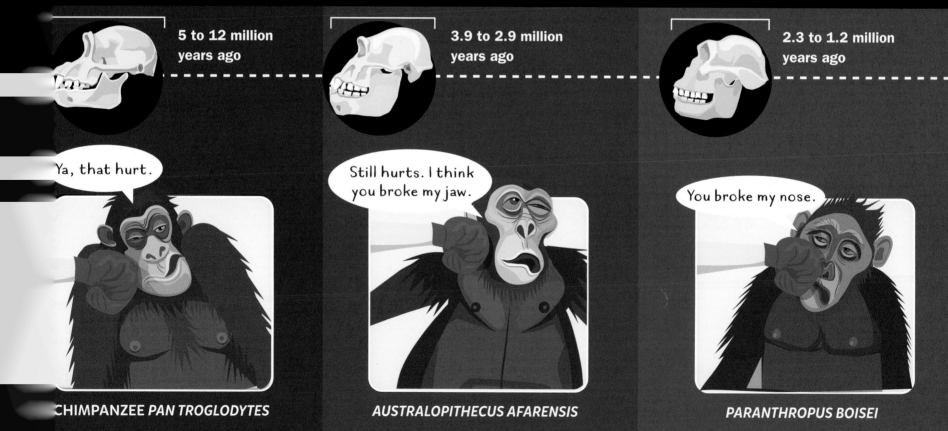

5 to 12 million years ago

3.9 to 2.9 million years ago

2.3 to 1.2 million years ago

Ya, that hurt.

Still hurts. I think you broke my jaw.

You broke my nose.

CHIMPANZEE *PAN TROGLODYTES*

AUSTRALOPITHECUS AFARENSIS

PARANTHROPUS BOISEI

opponent down, or stomp on them (also effective). If they do strike, they use the base of their palm with open fingers. That's when the science community asked the next logical quesiton. Which is better—smacking someone with your fist or your palm?

CADAVER ULTIMATE FIGHTING

To answer that question, they ordered some body parts and staged a cadaver beatdown. Using the dead arms, they compared punching a dumbbell with a closed fist vs. smacking it with an open fist. The study found that the closed fist was less likely to break bones in the hand and delivered 55 percent more of a wallop. This tells us two things:
1. Some scientists have ridiculously fun jobs, and
2. we might not have evolved to have opposable thumbs just to pick daisies and use tools.

chimpanzee   human

If our skulls evolved to withstand punches, maybe Bigfoot's skull **didn't** evolve because he is not a jerk.

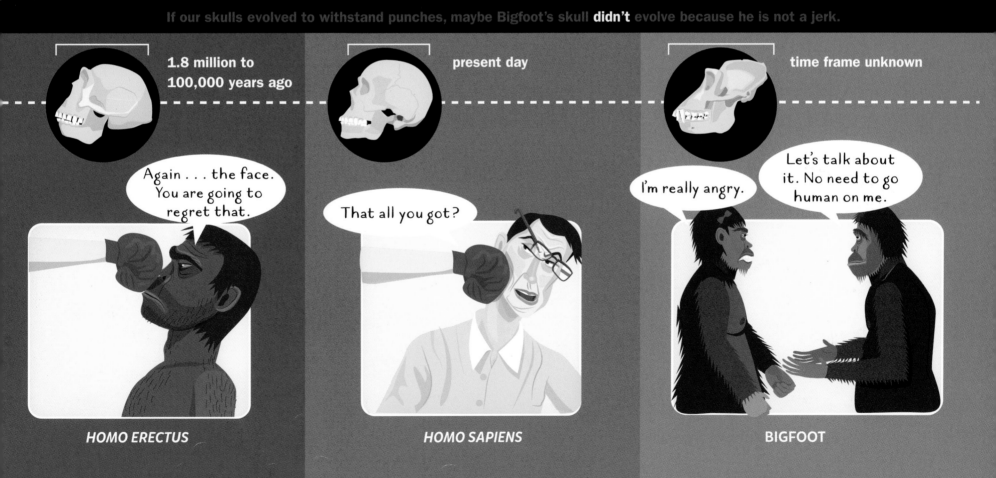

1.8 million to 100,000 years ago

Again . . . the face. You are going to regret that.

HOMO ERECTUS

present day

That all you got?

HOMO SAPIENS

time frame unknown

I'm really angry.

Let's talk about it. No need to go human on me.

BIGFOOT

HOW TO FIND BIGFOOT

A. HIDES IN FOREST
See the map on the next page to find where.

B. VOCALIZATION
May scream, wail, whoop, or whistle.

C. FAVORITE FOODS
Loves meat, fish, Kit Kat bars, and berries.

D. HAIRY
Has dark brown, black, reddish, or white hair.

E. MUSTY ODOR
Smells like putrid cabbage, rotting eggs, and dead skunk.

F. KNOCKS ON WOOD
Uses knocking as a sign of aggression.

G. LARGER THAN HUMANS
6 to 10 feet tall (1.8 to 3 m)
400 to 1,000 pounds (181 to 454 kg)

H. SCAT IN AREA
Scat is feces. Bigfoot scat resembles bear scat.

I. BIPEDAL
Walks on two legs.

J. LARGE FOOTPRINTS
Makes much larger footprints than humans do.

K. BUILDS NESTS
Makes from interwoven branches and leaves.

I'm not Bigfoot! I'm just a little skunk ape.

Orangutans and gorillas build similar nests.

BEST STATES TO FIND BIGFOOT

In the United States alone, the Bigfoot Field Researchers Organization has recorded over three thousand squatchy encounters, spanning every state except Hawaii (and Washington, DC). That's a lot of people seeing the same hairy, bipedal beast hiding in the forest. Is it possible that so many people could be just seeing a man in an ape suit?

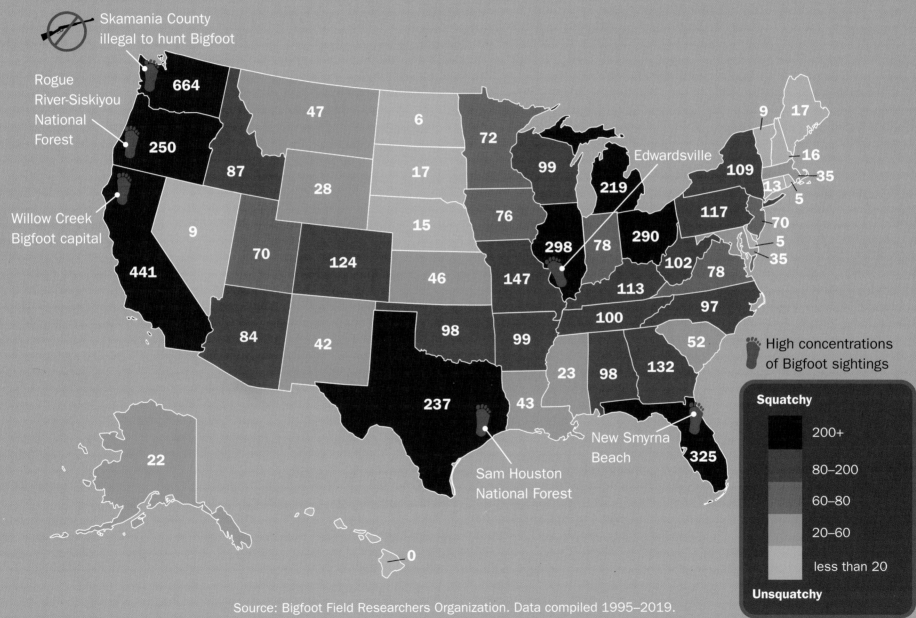

Skamania County illegal to hunt Bigfoot

Rogue River-Siskiyou National Forest

Willow Creek Bigfoot capital

664

250

87

47

6

72

99

109

9

17

16

35

13

5

28

17

219

117

76

290

102

70

124

15

298

78

441

46

147

113

78

97

84

42

98

99

100

52

237

43

23

98

132

22

New Smyrna Beach

325

Sam Houston National Forest

Edwardsville

High concentrations of Bigfoot sightings

0

Squatchy

200+

80–200

60–80

20–60

less than 20

Unsquatchy

Source: Bigfoot Field Researchers Organization. Data compiled 1995–2019.

ANIMAL FOOTPRINTS: IS IT SQUATCHY?

The first step in proving Bigfoot's existence is finding his footprint. Here are some examples of animals' prints so you can know if you have really found a Bigfoot footprint.

9 inches (23 cm)

CHIMPANZEE

12 to 16 inches (30 to 41 cm)

GRIZZLY BEAR (HIND LEGS)

6 to 9 inches (15 to 23 cm)

BLACK BEAR (HIND LEGS)

Chimpanzee
Known as knuckle walkers, chimpanzees can only walk upright for short periods of time. Most Bigfoot sightings claim the beast walks upright. A chimp's foot also has an opposable thumb for grasping tree branches. Most Bigfoot prints lack this thumb.

front leg

hind leg

Bear Prints vs. Bigfoot
You can tell a bear print from a Bigfoot print by the way the hind and front leg prints are different. Bear prints are often mistaken for Bigfoot prints if the hind leg and front leg prints overlap, making it appear as if it is one large footprint.

Bigfoot vs. Human
A Bigfoot print will be flat because Bigfoot lacks a defined arch.

16 inches
(41 cm)

BIGFOOT

10 inches
(25 cm)

HUMAN

14 inches
(36 cm)

GORILLA

Tip: Some of the clearest prints have been found near lakes and streams where heavy feet make clear impressions in the soft mud.

The size varies depending on the breed.

DOG

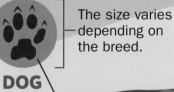

If Bigfoot tracks me, he may eat me.

A Nose for the Job
Dogs are great at tracking Bigfoot by his scent. Just don't let your dog get eaten.

HOW TO MAKE A PLASTER CAST OF A BIGFOOT FOOTPRINT

Once you find Bigfoot tracks, you must collect proof. The best way to record a Bigfoot track is to make a plaster cast of it.

TOOLS

2-INCH-WIDE (5 CM) PLASTIC STRIPS (cut from any large plastic bottle)

LATEX GLOVES

MIXING BOWL

WHISK

WATER

GYPSUM CEMENT

TROWEL

1. CLEAN THE PRINT.
Clean up any loose twigs or branches around the print. Remove them carefully so that you don't smear the print.

2. MARK OFF THE PRINT.
Encircle the print with the plastic strips. Use paper clips to extend the circle as needed.

3. MIX.
Wearing latex gloves, slowly stir together water and gypsum in a bowl until the mixture is the consistency of pancake batter. To remove any air bubbles, tap the bowl gently on the ground. If the ground is dry, add more water to your mixture so it is not too thick. You don't want the plaster to crush your print.

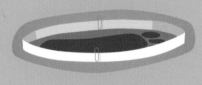

4. POUR
Gently pour the gypsum-and-water mixture over the print. Do not overfill.

5. WAIT. BE PATIENT.
Depending on the humidity, it can take up to 30 minutes to set.

6. REMOVE PLASTER.
Dig around the perimeter of the cast with a trowel, and then gently lift the plaster cast.

7. CURE.
Wrap in newspaper to cure.

HOW TO SURVIVE A BIGFOOT ATTACK

Although Bigfoot, like most bears and other wild animals, generally avoids humans, there is still a chance that you will be attacked by one on your next camping trip. Use the following tips to survive a Bigfoot attack.

1. KEEP A CLEAN CAMP.
Bigfoot has a keen sense of smell and may be attracted to leftover meals. Wash all utensils and seal uneaten food in airtight containers. Remove pet food from the campsite. Remember, Bigfoot likes to eat dogs.

2. KNOW THE AREA.
Refer to the Bigfoot map of sightings (p. 113) to avoid any unwanted Bigfoot encounters.

3. MAKE LOUD NOISES.
Bang on pots and pans, yell, or blow on a horn. Bigfoot is often scared off by loud noises.

4. DO NOT MAKE ANY SUDDEN MOVEMENTS.
This will threaten Bigfoot and cause him to attack. Most attacks from animals such as grizzly bears are defensive attacks. Do not run. Running or exposing your back will prompt Bigfoot to attack.

5. DO NOT MAKE EYE CONTACT.
Most wild animals such as grizzly bears see eye contact as an act of aggression, which will prompt them to attack.

6. DO NOT PLAY WITH BABY BIGFOOTS.
If you spot a baby Bigfoot, you might be tempted to play with it, especially if it is cute and furry. Don't. Bigfoots are very protective of their young, and nothing will get them to attack faster than messing with their children.

* Please note: These tips can also be used to survive grizzly bear attacks.

117

REAL MONSTERS: MYTH OR SPECIES?

Scientists call animals like Bigfoot whose existence has yet to be proven to mainstream science cryptids. The following animals were once thought to be mythological creatures or extinct because they went undetected for centuries.

1797
PLATYPUS

When a four-legged creature with the body of a fat, short-legged cat; the tail of a beaver; and a seemingly misplaced bill was discovered in 1797, we can understand why scientists collectively shook their heads in disbelief. Two decades later, the naturalist Robert Knox called it a "freak imposture." Freakish it may be, but no animal would intentionally choose to look that ridiculous.

1869
GIANT PANDA

Even in their homeland of China, pandas were once believed to be as mythical as Bigfoot. The problem was that just like Bigfoot, pandas were really good at hiding. The first proof of their existence came in 1869 when French missionary Armand David sent a panda skin back to Europe. For the next sixty years, scientists tried to capture a live panda but were unsuccessful. Then, in 1936, socialite Ruth Harkness found a baby panda in northern China and brought him back to a Chicago zoo. Today, the giant pandas are a huge zoo attraction, and the National Zoo's giant panda Mei Xiang has become so popular that she even has her own Instagram hashtag (#MeiXiang). Not bad for a bear people didn't believe existed.

For decades after their discovery, scientists thought pandas were a species of raccoon until DNA analysis revealed they were actually bears.

The odd four-legged relative of the giraffe can lick its eyeballs with its tongue, avoid poisons by eating charcoal, and hide extremely well.

1901
OKAPI

The okapi proves Mother Nature can be fickle. She may have started to make a zebra but then changed her mind after she finished putting stripes on the butt. The okapi is so odd-looking that no one believed the Congo natives when they claimed there was a bizarre-looking half zebra, half giraffe creature hiding in the rain forest. It wasn't until 1901 when Harry Johnston discovered one that the mythical okapi was declared a species.

118

1902
MOUNTAIN GORILLA

A hairy, manlike beast that hides from humans? Well, that is as silly as Bigfoot. At least that was what Westerners thought when they heard Africans tell stories of "wild men." No one believed the stories until 1902, when Captain Friedrich Robert von Beringe discovered these supposed wild men and gave them the proper name of *Gorilla beringei*.

Me neither.

No one believes I am real.

1910
KOMODO DRAGON

If one of your friends claimed she saw a 10-foot (3 m) dragon eat a man whole, you probably would say, "Puhleeeeeease." Islanders of Komodo told similar tales of the *ora buaya darat*, which means "land crocodile," but no one took them seriously. Then Komodo dragon specimens were discovered in 1910, and American trophy hunters became determined to put a dragon on their walls. In 1926, an expedition led by William Douglas Burden on the island of Rinca brought back two live Komodo dragons to the Bronx Zoo. Unfortunately, the scientists had no clue how to care for a giant lizard/dragon creature, so the pair of Komodo dragons died shortly after they arrived.

1938
COELACANTH

When a species is believed to have gone extinct and then suddenly reappears in the fossil record, it is called a **Lazarus taxon**. The term derives from the biblical story of Lazarus of Bethany, who came back to life after being dead for four days. One such creature that was believed to be extinct was the armored, bottom-dwelling fish known as the coelacanth (pronounced SEE-luh-kanth). The coelacanth can reach more than 6 feet long (1.8 m) and weigh over 200 pounds (91 kg). That's not the strange part. They also have a hinged jaw (with teeth), a tiny brain, and a heart shaped like a tube. They were believed to have gone extinct sixty-six million years ago during the great dinosaur extinction, until they were discovered in 1938 off the coast of East London, South Africa.

Despite looking like a fish, the coelacanth is more closely related to mammals such as humans. You also don't want to eat one. It is slimy, covered with mucus, and full of urea—the protein excreted in urine.

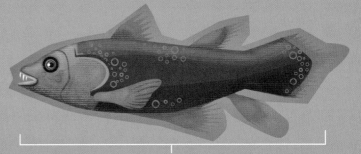

6 feet (2 m)

GODZILLA
KING OF THE MONSTERS!

When Japanese audiences first saw *Godzilla* in 1954, they left the theater in tears. They didn't weep out of fright or the ridiculousness of a 60,000-ton (54,430 t) radioactive dinosaur stomping all over Tokyo. They wept because Godzilla was a monster born out of a very real tragedy.

In the summer of 1945, World War II had ended in Europe, but America and its allies were still at war with Japan. In the upcoming months, the predicted loss of life was a staggering fifty thousand more American soldiers. With many Americans weary of war, US president Harry S. Truman decided to use the most destructive weapon ever created: the atomic bomb.

On August 6, 1945, the US dropped an atomic bomb on Hiroshima, Japan, killing roughly eighty thousand people instantly—the highest death toll ever from a weapon of mass destruction. Another forty thousand people would perish when a second bomb was dropped on Nagasaki three days later.

In the movie, Godzilla's atomic breath sprays out like a water hose and sets buildings on fire. The reality of atomic warfare was much more frightening. Those close to where the bomb struck were immediately incinerated. Sometimes, the only mark left behind was a dark stain on the ground and walls called a "nuclear shadow." These shadows outlined where people once stood, as if their bodies still blocked the rays of the sun. Those who did survive said that at the moment the bomb flashed overhead, they could see the bones in their fingers, like an X-ray.

After the bombs detonated, residual radioactive material continued to fall from the sky as "black rain"—a sticky, dark rain that stained clothing and skin an inky black. This **fallout** contributed to a new illness: radiation sickness. People suffering from radiation sickness experienced diarrhea, vomiting, hair loss, and throat sores. Some eventually died.

Japan surrendered six days after the bombing of Nagasaki, and Americans celebrated the end of the war. In the following years, the Japanese people rebuilt their cities, but reminders of the devastation were everywhere. Many survivors were left with scars, their faces and limbs riddled with burns and **keloid scars**—large bumps of scar tissue that inspired Godzilla's bumpy skin. Other reminders were hidden deep in the bone marrow and the blood vessels of survivors. Years later, some Japanese people were blinded by cataracts or developed malignant cancers. Survivors of the bomb, called *hibakusha*, carried on with their lives, but they would never forget.

WHAT IS AN ATOMIC BOMB?

Atomic bombs create a chain reaction with the nuclei of certain atoms (either uranium or plutonium), which results in a tremendous explosion. The explosion gives off energy in the form of heat, light, and **ionizing radiation**, which has significant short-term and long-term effects on living things and the environment.

121

GODZILLA RISES FROM THE ATOMIC ASHES

Like most stories of great powers unleashed, the history of the atomic bomb does not end there. From 1946 to 1958, several hydrogen bomb tests were conducted on the twenty-three islands of Bikini Atoll. On March 1, 1954, one such test, named Castle Bravo, would give birth to Godzilla.

The US government had predicted the bomb would have a 5- to 6-megaton yield. They were wrong. Really wrong. The bomb exploded with a 15-megaton yield—a force of 750 to 1,000 Hiroshima bombs. The bomb vaporized the test island, two nearby islands, and left a mile-wide (1.6 km) crater on the lagoon floor.

At 6:45 a.m., the fishing boat *Lucky Dragon No. 5* was casting its nets about 85 miles (137 km) outside of the Castle Bravo test site—well out of reach of the expected detonation. Suddenly, a flash of light turned the horizon bright yellow as if the sun had exploded and leaked out of the sky.

Two hours later, the air was thick with fog and white flakes rained down on the crew, covering the deck. Amused, the fishermen held out their tongues to catch the falling snowflakes. Except it wasn't snow.

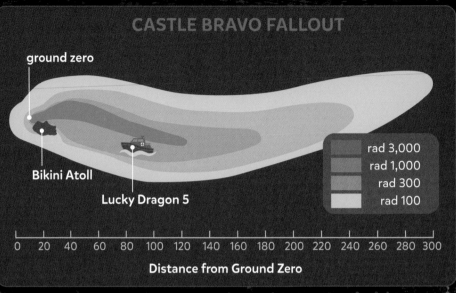

CASTLE BRAVO FALLOUT

ground zero

Bikini Atoll

Lucky Dragon 5

rad 3,000
rad 1,000
rad 300
rad 100

0 20 40 60 80 100 120 140 160 180 200 220 240 260 280 300

Distance from Ground Zero

*Accumulated doses of radiation measured ninety-six hours after detonation

Atolls are large, ring-shaped reefs. Even today, the remaining islands are uninhabitable because of the dangerous radiation levels.

What would later be known as "ashes of death" was radioactive calcium from vaporized coral. In the following days, the crew became violently ill with vomiting, severe eye pain, burnt skin, headaches, diarrhea, and fever—classic symptoms of radiation sickness. Crew member Aikichi Kuboyama died 206 days later, and several fishermen died over the following years. Kuboyama's last words on his deathbed were, "I pray that I am the last victim of an atomic or hydrogen bomb."

The inhabitants of the Marshall Islands were evacuated days later as the fallout continued to spread. Fifteen islands and atolls were contaminated by Castle Bravo. To this day, it is the largest thermonuclear device ever detonated by the United States.

1954: MAKING GODZILLA

In the original movie, Godzilla is a gigantic underwater dinosaur from the Cretaceous period. The monster is asleep in a cave in the Pacific Ocean until he is awakened from his slumber by the hydrogen bombs exploding around him. His most dangerous weapon is not his size but his "atomic breath," which streams out of his mouth as a nuclear blast. A lot of screaming and stomping follows, but no army can kill the monster until scientists invent an "oxygen destroyer."

In creating Godzilla, Director Ishirō Honda wanted to make a monster movie that made the dangers of "radiation visible." To make Godzilla seem more real, he shot the film like a documentary with darkened scenes of screaming people and buildings collapsing under Godzilla's fiery breath that appeared ripped straight from war footage.

The creators of Godzilla could have used **stop-motion** animation similar to how King Kong was made, but it would have taken years, and they had a deadline of six months. Instead, Honda chose to use a newly invented technique called suitmation where actor Haruo Nakajima would play the part of the monster inside a suit. This is not as easy as it sounds. It was so hot inside the suit that he often fainted from the heat, and sometimes he tripped and could not get up.

I need sunblock!

WHAT DO GODZILLA AND BATHING SUITS HAVE IN COMMON?

The atomic bomb not only inspired one of the biggest movie monster legends, but also a tiny piece of fashion—the bikini. The bikini was invented by French designer Louis Réard, who named it after the atomic bombs being tested on Bikini Atoll. Réard predicted his swimwear would be just as explosive. He was right about that one. When the bikini was first worn in America, several states banned it for being immodest and most swimsuit models refused to wear it. It took a few movie stars, or "bombshells," adopting the fashion for it to be acceptable beachwear.

While it may seem a callous name for a fashion design, at the time, the American public was not fully aware of the destruction caused by the atomic bomb. With the exception of the bomb's mushroom cloud ascending into the sky, film footage showing the aftermath of Hiroshima was not released until twenty-five years later.

Godzilla's gray, bumpy skin was meant to resemble the keloid scars of the atomic bomb victims. Later renditions of Godzilla portrayed him as green instead of gray.

THE ANATOMY OF GODZILLA
SCIENCE VS. FICTION

B. SMALL BRAIN
doesn't need to solve math equations

C. BRAIN SPONGE
reduces the pressure before the blood enters the brain

A. FORWARD-FACING EYES
for wide field of vision

D. FOUR-FINGERED CLAWS
for tearing up buildings

E. POWERFUL NECK MUSCLES
for swallowing kids whole

Q. SHARP TEETH
for chomping on school buses

F. AIR SACS
to pump blood more efficiently and breathe at high altitudes

P. DEAFENING ROAR
sounds like a dying elephant

G. OSTEODERMS
armored skin to resist attacks

O. ATOMIC BREATH
to destroy cities

N. GILLS
to breathe underwater

M. LUNGS
to breathe on land

L. THREE FOUR-CHAMBERED HEARTS
two hearts pumping blood to gills; third, larger heart pumping blood through the body

K. LARGE STOMACH
for digesting King Kong slowly

J. BIPEDAL
walks on two legs

I. CARTILAGE PLATES AND SQUISHY JOINTS
for bearing weight

H. SHOCK-ABSORBING PADS
to stomp on houses

To create Godzilla, his designers drew inspiration from dinosaurs like *Tyrannosaurus rex*, *Iguanodon*, and *Stegosaurus*. Because dinosaurs are extinct, it is hard to tell if Godzilla's anatomy is possible, but there are some things we know about dinosaurs that make the King of the Monsters less or more believable.

GODZILLA'S SIZE

Just like King Kong (p. 56), Godzilla would turn into mush if he tried to move due to the square-cube law. Godzilla is estimated to weigh approximately 60,000 tons (54,430 t). The largest known dinosaur to ever stomp around was *Argentinosaurus*, and it was less than 100 tons (91 t).

GODZILLA'S STRUT

Forget the dancing Godzilla scenes, no dinosaur walked like Godzilla. Godzilla is bipedal—he walks on two legs **(J)**. Bipedal dinosaurs like *T. rex* always had a backbone parallel to the ground and balanced their upper half by using their tail as a counterweight. Scientists believe they ran with a hip-rolling motion by throwing their weight forward while keeping their tail raised for balance. (They actually probably looked more like a chicken strutting than a monster stomping.) In contrast, Godzilla moves with his spine in an upright position and with his tail down. At his size, this would be a great way to topple over.

GODZILLA'S SKIN

Several dinosaurs were covered with thick armor similar to Godzilla's. These bony plates are called **osteoderms (G)**. They were found in dinosaurs like the *Ankylosaurus* and Stegosaurus but can also be found today in animals such as crocodiles, armadillos, and some lizards.

GODZILLA IS A FAINTER

Due to Godzilla's immense size, his heart is too far from his brain. As soon as he lowers his head to chomp on a bus and then lifts it back up, the blood would not reach his brain in time and he would faint. (This is why you sometimes get dizzy if you get up too quickly.) Godzilla would need a network of elastic blood vessels called a rete mirabile, or blood sponge **(C)**. Giraffes have a blood sponge, which acts like a series of valves regulating how much blood can enter the brain so the giraffe can lower and then raise its head without fainting.

GODZILLA'S ROAR

One of Godzilla's scariest features is his roar **(P)**, but most dinosaurs did not sound like a dying elephant. Scientists suspect many dinosaurs squawked like a chicken or even cooed because they are related to today's birds. Birds can't roar because their sounds comes out of a fluid-filled cavity near the heart called a syrinx, while animals that roar (including humans) have a larynx (voice box). Dinosaurs similar to Godzilla had a syrinx, not a larynx.

OSTEODERMS

WHAT KIND OF DINOSAUR IS GODZILLA?

When anthropologists discover a dinosaur fossil, one of the first questions they ask is, what did it eat? Dinosaurs are classified as either carnivores (meat eaters), herbivores (plant eaters), omnivores (plant and meat eaters), or insectivores (insect eaters).* Godzilla supposedly doesn't need food because he feeds off radiation, but his skull tells a different story.

Eating only radiation gets boring.

Uh-oh

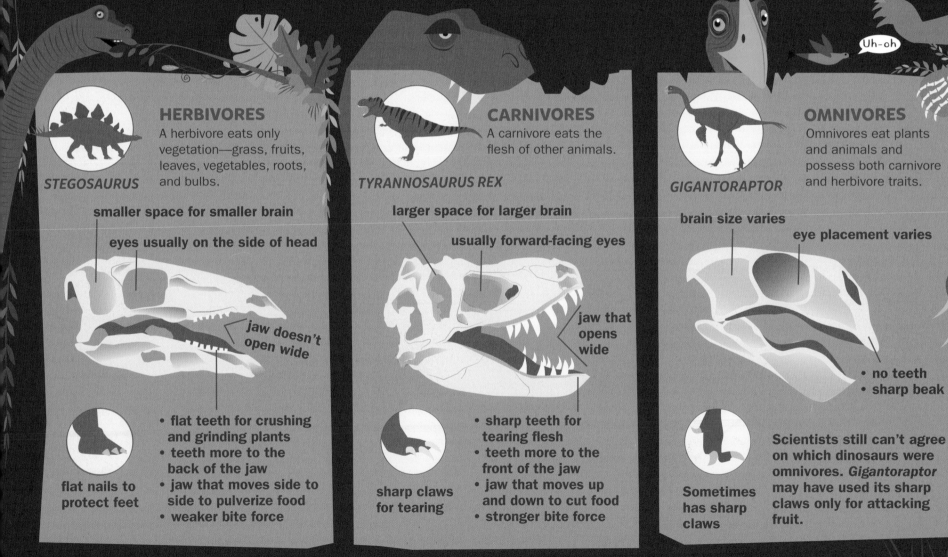

HERBIVORES

A herbivore eats only vegetation—grass, fruits, leaves, vegetables, roots, and bulbs.

STEGOSAURUS

- smaller space for smaller brain
- eyes usually on the side of head
- jaw doesn't open wide
- flat nails to protect feet

• flat teeth for crushing and grinding plants
• teeth more to the back of the jaw
• jaw that moves side to side to pulverize food
• weaker bite force

CARNIVORES

A carnivore eats the flesh of other animals.

TYRANNOSAURUS REX

- larger space for larger brain
- usually forward-facing eyes
- jaw that opens wide
- sharp claws for tearing

• sharp teeth for tearing flesh
• teeth more to the front of the jaw
• jaw that moves up and down to cut food
• stronger bite force

OMNIVORES

Omnivores eat plants and animals and possess both carnivore and herbivore traits.

GIGANTORAPTOR

- brain size varies
- eye placement varies
- no teeth
- sharp beak
- Sometimes has sharp claws

Scientists still can't agree on which dinosaurs were omnivores. *Gigantoraptor* may have used its sharp claws only for attacking fruit.

* Although there were small insectivore dinosaurs, there are not enough cockroaches to feed a dinosaur of Godzilla's size.

GODZILLA LIKES MEAT

Godzilla's skull indicates that he is a carnivore similar to dinosaurs such as *Carnotaurus*, *Ceratosaurus*, or *Tyrannosaurus rex*. Godzilla was most likely a theropod dinosaur. All theropods had lightweight skulls, sharp teeth, a wide jaw, and bipedal ability. See the size comparison below for how much of a meal other dinosaurs would be for Godzilla.

WHICH OF THE FOLLOWING EAT MEAT?

VENUS FLYTRAP   **DEER**   **GIANT PANDA**

ANSWER: They all do. You probably guessed by the sharp teeth that the Venus flytrap was a meat eater but, yes, even Bambi can turn into a flesh-eating beast. Deer have been found to eat dead rabbits, fish, and occasionally steak off grills. And while pandas may spend most of their day chomping down on bamboo, 1 percent of their diet is an occasional flesh feast. Scientists don't know why herbivores sometimes eat meat. It could be because they are deficient in certain vitamins, or it could be because animals that have a varied diet are more likely to adapt and survive—sort of an evolutionary form of keeping your options open.

164 FT.
(50 M)

15 TO 20 FT.
(5 TO 6 M)

16 FT.
(5 M)

9 FT.
(3 M)

HOW DOES GODZILLA BREATHE?

Godzilla lives in his underwater cave until humans make him mad enough to come onto land. But how does Godzilla breathe on land? Whether you are a fish or a prehistoric dinosaur, every animal needs oxygen to breathe. Fish use gills to pull oxygen out of the water, while mammals, most adult amphibians, and reptiles use lungs to pull oxygen from the air. How can Godzilla do both?

The pollution is killing me!

LUNGS

Most reptiles and mammals use lungs to take oxygen from the air and then expel carbon dioxide when breathing out. (Lungs can only take oxygen from the air, not from water.) Mammals and reptiles need much more oxygen than cold-blooded amphibians, Luckily, air has twenty times more oxygen than water does.

GILLS AND LUNGS

The African lungfish uses gills to breathe underwater and lungs to breathe air at the surface of the water. If kept wet, the lungfish can survive out of water for two years. Maybe Godzilla uses both too?

GILLS

Fish use gills to take dissolved oxygen from the water and then expel carbon dioxide.

SKIN

Some amphibians such as arboreal salamanders have neither gills nor lungs. Instead, they breathe through their skin and the membranes in their mouth and throat. But lungs are a much more efficient way for large creatures like Godzilla to breathe because they provide a larger surface area to get oxygen. As a comparison, the surface area of your skin is 16.1 to 21.5 square feet (1.5 to 2 sq. m), while your lungs have a surface area of 540 to 810 square feet (50 to 75 sq. m).

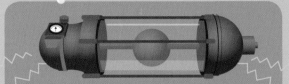

THE OXYGEN DESTROYER

Godzilla was killed by the Oxygen Destroyer which, just as it sounds, destroyed all the oxygen in the water. What would happen if there wasn't enough oxygen in the water? Because warm-blooded animals need more oxygen than cold-blooded animals, whales and dolphins would be the first to die, followed by cold-blooded fish. Land creatures would also suffer. If we took away all the oxygen from the earth's water (H_2O), it would become hydrogen gas (H_2) and explode every living cell in every living creature, including humans on land. And just like after breathing in helium from a balloon, our screams would sound ridiculous.

MAYBE GODZILLA HOLDS HIS BREATH?

It is also possible that Godzilla uses lungs to hold his breath underwater and then comes to the surface for air. The following mammals and reptiles give us some clues as to how long a prehistoric dinosaur could hold his breath and hide in his underwater cave.

> I can even eat underwater. Maybe Godzilla can too . . .

HUMAN
1 to 2 MINUTES
In 2016 Aleix Segura Vendrell broke the world record for holding his breath underwater: 24 minutes, 3.45 seconds. But most humans can't come anywhere close to this.

HIPPO
5 MINUTES
Hippos stay underwater longer by closing their nostrils.

DOLPHIN
20 MINUTES
Marine mammals' red blood cells carry more oxygen, which allows them to hold their breath underwater longer.

CROCODILE
60 MINUTES
Crocodiles stay underwater longer by closing heart valves and slowing down their metabolism.

WHALE
90 MINUTES
Sperm whales take long dives by using a protein called myoglobin to bind oxygen in their blood.

GODZILLA
UNLIMITED MINUTES
Godzilla can survive underwater until the oxygen destroyer kills him.

HOW SCARY IS GODZILLA'S ATOMIC BREATH?

IONIZING RADIATION

Everything from this book to your hand holding it is made up of tiny atoms too small to see without a powerful microscope. Atoms are held together by protons, neutrons, and electrons. When Godzilla belches his fiery breath, he uses the same radiation as an atomic bomb to disintegrate the center of the atom, called the nucleus. In addition, Godzilla uses a type of short wavelength radiation called ionizing radiation. High levels of ionizing radiation are dangerous because they can incinerate your body in seconds or cause cancer or birth defects in those exposed.

Not all radiation causes death and destruction. Non-ionizing radiation includes visible and ultraviolet light and radio-frequency waves. This type of radiation gives you rainbows and allows you to watch your favorite TV shows. It is called non-ionizing radiation because it is not powerful enough to remove an electron from an atom. It is strong enough to move atoms to heat food (microwaves) or emit light (televisions).

Ionizing radiation inside an atom
Atoms contain a nucleus with positively charged protons and neutrons without any charge. Surrounding the nucleus is a cloud of negatively charged electrons that balance the positive charge and hold the atom together. When exposed to ionizing radiation, electrons are kicked out of an atom, which causes the atoms to become unstable. That's when bad things happen, like nuclear explosions, three-headed dogs, or radioactive dinosaurs.

NON-IONIZING RADIATION

less energy   long wavelengths   no biological radiation

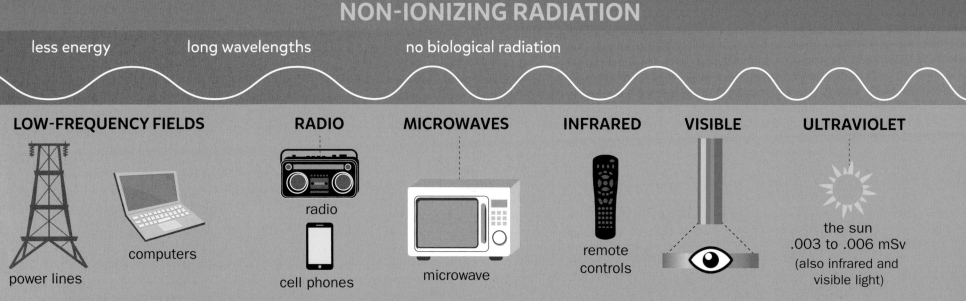

| LOW-FREQUENCY FIELDS | RADIO | MICROWAVES | INFRARED | VISIBLE | ULTRAVIOLET |

power lines   computers   radio   cell phones   microwave   remote controls   the sun .003 to .006 mSv (also infrared and visible light)

NOT SCARY TO SOME . . .

MARIE CURIE VS. GODZILLA

Science has yet to witness a giant radioactive monster, but some radioactive elements can be found in nature. For example, radium and polonium were discovered by physicist and chemist Marie Curie in 1896. She observed that these elements gave off strong glowing rays and called it "radioactivity." Her pioneering research led to her becoming the first woman to win a Nobel Prize. She later set up the Radium Institute to use radiation to help treat people with cancer. Marie Curie died from aplastic anemia in 1934 due to radiation exposure from her own experiments. Godzilla did not make his movie debut until after her death, but most likely she would have taken him on too.

MEASURING RADIATION

Today, we measure how much radiation something is giving off with the becquerel (Bq). To measure exposure to radiation over time, we use the sievert (Sv), the smaller millisievert (mSv), or the even smaller microsievert (μSv). Low levels of radiation are not dangerous. The average person is exposed to almost 3 mSv of background radiation a year from things in our environment such as soil, water, sunlight, food, and even the natural radioactivity inside our bodies. Problems arise when we are exposed to too much radiation at once.

"Nothing in life is to be feared. It is to be understood."
—Marie Curie

88 7s²
Ra
Radium
(226)

84
Po
Polonium
(209)

...... **MARIE CURIE**
(not afraid of Godzilla)

her body inside
...... her coffin
257 to 360
Bq/m³

IONIZING RADIATION

radioactive   short wavelengths   more energy

BACKGROUND RADIATION   **COSMIC**   **X-RAYS**   **GAMMA RAYS**

soil water heat
3.1 mSv per year

eating a
banana
.1 μSv

a flight from
New York to LA
.04 mSv

chest X-ray
.1 mSv

CT scan
10 mSv

Hiroshima center
155 Sv/hr
1 mile (1.6 km)
from Hiroshima
360 mSv/hr.

radiation sickness
1 to 3 Sv/hr.

Chernobyl explosion
490 mSv/hr.

death
6 to 10 Sv/hr.

Godzilla's
breath
300+ Sv/hr.

WHERE GODZILLA SHOULD REFUEL
THE MOST RADIOACTIVE PLACES IN THE WORLD

Although Godzilla chomps on an occasional screaming human, he needs radiation to survive. In humans, areas with high radiation can cause cancer, birth defects, or eventually death. So while you may want to avoid these places, our prehistoric monster can relax, refuel, and get his daily dose of monster health.

SELLAFIELD, CUMBRIA, UK

Irish Sea
61 Bq/m³

CHERNOBYL, PRIPYAT, UKRAINE
8.76 mSv a year

THE POLYGON, KAZAKHSTAN
70–4,470 mSv a year

FUKUSHIMA, JAPAN
20 mSv a year

HARRISBURG, PA, USA

HANFORD, WA, USA

Mediterranean Sea
1.7 Bq/m³

RAMSAR, IRAN
260 mSv a year

MAILUU-SUU, KYRGYZSTAN

YANGJIANG, CHINA
5.4 mSv a year

KERALA, INDIA
35 mSv a year

GUARAPARI, BRAZIL
35 mSv a year

■ Unsafe levels
■ Levels not reported
■ Background radiation
■ Cesium- 137*

*Cesium levels are from background radiation and nuclear test sites.

Radiation levels change per hour and are listed as estimates.

There are an estimated fifteen thousand nuclear warheads in the world today. Most are more powerful than Godzilla's breath.

CHERNOBYL, UKRAINE

On April 27, 1986, Russian officials evacuated the town of Pripyat due to an explosion at the Chernobyl nuclear plant. They told residents to take only important papers because they would return in a few days. That estimate was a bit off. According to most scientists, radiation levels will be safe for people to return to their homes in twenty-four thousand years. The biggest nuclear disaster to date, Chernobyl exploded and had a fallout greater than four hundred Hiroshima bombs. One plant worker was immediately incinerated, another died in the hospital, and many more people died as result of radiation sickness.

FUKUSHIMA, JAPAN

On March 11, 2011, an earthquake followed by a tsunami caused a meltdown at the Fukushima nuclear plant. While there were no deaths caused directly by the meltdown, nineteen thousand three hundred people died from the earthquake and tsunami, and ninety thousand people were forced to evacuate their homes due to fear of radiation poisoning. In 2015 residents were allowed to return to Fukushima, but few did. In 2017 robots recorded radiation outside the reactor at 530 sieverts per hour—enough to kill a human in seconds.

THE POLYGON, KAZAKHSTAN

When the massive mushroom cloud loomed above the village of Sarzhal in eastern Kazakhstan and the surrounding region, people were unaware of the nuclear fallout that rained down on them. Instead, they were ordered outside their homes and then examined by doctors. From 1949–1989, the Soviet Union conducted 456 atomic explosions, using the residents as unwitting guinea pigs. The radiation levels have caused numerous cases of thyroid diseases, cancer, and deformities. One in every twenty children in the area is born with a birth defect, including spine abnormalities, developmental issues, and microcephaly—a rare condition where the head is abnormally small.

SELLAFIELD, UK

On October 10, 1957, the Sellafield plant caught fire, causing the worst nuclear accident in Britain's history. Today, the waste continues to contaminate the Irish Sea along with England, Scotland, and Scandinavian fisheries. Many Swedish fishermen have complained about birth defects in the marine life. (A six-legged octopus was found in one fisherman's net.) One study even found radioactive plutonium in British kids' teeth.

RAMSAR, IRAN

Known for its magical healing hot springs, there is something else in the water in Ramsar—radium. Ramsar has the highest level of background radiation levels in the world, which is caused mostly by radium-266. Raidum-266 usually causes lung cancer, but residents of Ramsar actually have lower rates of lung cancer (so far). Some scientists have theorized that being exposed to high levels of natural-occurring radiation has made the residents more resistant to radioactivity. Either way, this is Godzilla's favorite place to bathe.

HANFORD, WA, USA

Built during World War II, the Hanford plant once processed the plutonium that was used in the first nuclear bomb. Today, it is considered the most contaminated site in the United States. Efforts are now being made to dismantle and contain all radioactive materials over the next fifty years. Let's hope this gets done soon. Just one stomp from Godzilla would release enough plutonium into the atmosphere to be radioactive for a half million years.

I love my radioactive baths.

HOW TO SURVIVE GODZILLA'S NUCLEAR BREATH

You don't want to be squashed or eaten by Godzilla, but you also must avoid his nuclear breath. Godzilla's breath is strong enough to burn through concrete and melt steel, but the real danger is in the **nuclear fallout**—the residual radioactive material that will continue to "fall out" of the sky. This fallout is like a deadly, invisible dust that settles on anything in its range. The following tips will help you survive a Godzilla nuclear fallout:

1. WEAR WHITE. If you know Godzilla is coming to your town, wear white. Dark clothes absorb more radiation.

2. COVER YOUR EYES. Do not look at the blast from his breath. It will blind you in seconds.

3. STAY LOW. If you cannot find shelter, stay low to the ground and cover your head with your hands and arms.

4. RUN. The farther you can get away from Godzilla's nuclear breath, the better chance you have to survive.

5. SEEK SHELTER. In the event of a nuclear fallout, the United States Environmental Protection Agency (EPA) recommends that you first find shelter. Find a brick or concrete building, and go to the lowest floor, preferably underground. Then seal all windows and doors. Most important: stay in your shelter for at least two weeks. This is the average length of time that radioactive fallout will last (See zombie preparedness kit for what you need to have in any shelter, p. 53.)

WHERE TO FIND SHELTER

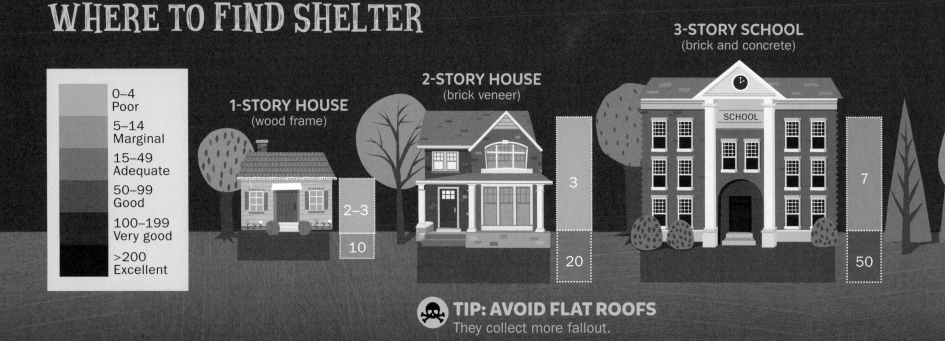

0–4 Poor
5–14 Marginal
15–49 Adequate
50–99 Good
100–199 Very good
>200 Excellent

1-STORY HOUSE (wood frame) — 2–3 / 10

2-STORY HOUSE (brick veneer) — 3 / 20

3-STORY SCHOOL (brick and concrete) — 7 / 50

TIP: AVOID FLAT ROOFS
They collect more fallout.

6. GET NAKED. When completely clear of the contaminated area, remove your outer layer of clothing to reduce exposure from radioactive material that may have fallen on your clothes. Wash all exposed body parts including your hair. Do not use conditioner because it will bind the radiation to your hair.

7. TAKE POTASSIUM IODINE. It will prevent your thyroid from absorbing radiation.

5-STORY BUILDING
(brick and concrete)

10
20
10
100

10-STORY BUILDING
(steel set in concrete)

	10
	20
50	30
	20
	10
	20
100	30
	20
	10
	200

I like to eat the fools in their cars first.

☠ **TIP: STAY CLEAR OF WINDOWS**
Move to the center of the building where there is less chance of radiation exposure from the outside.

☠ **TIP: DON'T GET IN YOUR CAR**
After a nuclear fallout, many vehicles will not work due to electromagnetic pulse (EMP). EMPs are bursts of invisible energy that destroy nearby electronics.

REAL MONSTERS: TRUE TALES OF RADIOACTIVE CREATURES

Godzilla is not the only radioactive animal wreaking havoc on the population. The following creatures have also been found to have dangerous levels of radioactivity:

THE WOLVES OF CHERNOBYL

In the "dead zone" close to where Chernobyl exploded, you won't find many humans, but you will find wolves . . . and lots of them. While humans cannot live in the area due to high levels of radiation, there are seven times more wolves than before the explosion. Scientists are now studying these animals in their strange apocalyptic settings to figure out why they are thriving. Some scientists have even theorized that without humans around, the wolves couldn't be happier.

THE RED FOREST

After the Chernobyl meltdown, the pine trees in a nearby forest turned bright red after dying. But radioactive trees are not the only reason to stay out of the forest. Birds that go in come out with smaller brains and deformed beaks. Insects such as butterflies, grasshoppers, and bees have dwindled. Strangest of all, the trees and leaves are not decaying at a normal rate. Scientists fear if the trees do not decay, the debris could cause one massive forest fire.

NUCLEAR PROTEST COWS

After the Fukushima nuclear meltdown, the Japanese government ordered all cows in the area to be killed. Fortunately, Japanese rancher Masami Yoshizawa had a soft spot for radioactive cows. He renamed his ranch the Ranch of Hope and rounded up the abandoned livestock to live in peace. And although Yoshizawa worries about his exposure to radioactivity (just being around the cows is dangerous), he chose to keep them alive as a reminder of the devastation caused by nuclear disasters.

GEIGER COUNTER CATS

We know Godzilla is radioactive because his breath glows blue, but radioactivity is invisible. A group of scientists realized this might be a problem for future generations who need to be warned when an area has unsafe levels. The solution: ray cats. Scientists hope to insert a gene for glowing into the household cat and then engineer the glowing to only turn on when exposed to radiation. So if you see your kitty suddenly look like a glowworm, you might want to get out of the area.

RADIOACTIVE RABBITS

In 2010 the people of Hanford, Washington, got a visit from a very special bunny. The rabbit was not dining on carrots but radioactive cesium and then dropping its radioactive turds across the area. Scientists believe it was most likely infected through the abandoned nuclear plant's water supply. And rabbits multiply much faster than angry dinosaurs.

NOT-SO-TASTY HAM

When the Chernobyl plant exploded, it sent a cloud of radioactive material across northern and central Sweden. Scientists believe the wild boar in the area became contaminated by eating radioactive wild mushrooms deep in the ground. Because most residents prefer not to eat radioactive ham, boar populations have multiplied and become a menace to farmers trying to protect their crops.

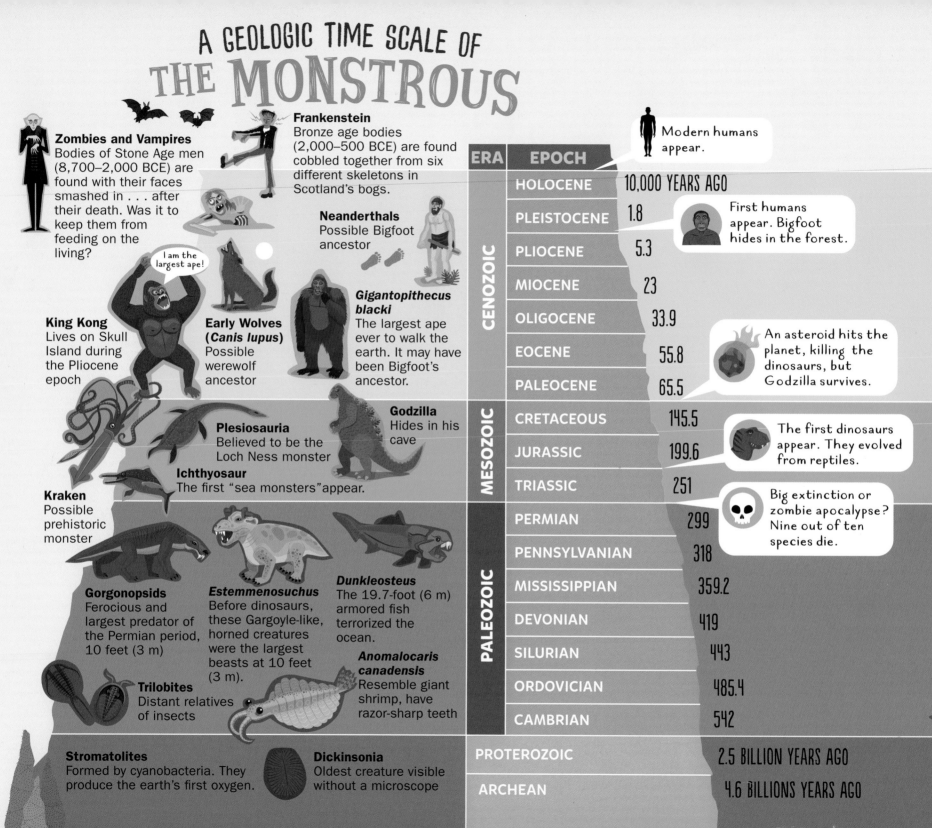

A GEOLOGIC TIME SCALE OF THE MONSTROUS

Zombies and Vampires
Bodies of Stone Age men (8,700–2,000 BCE) are found with their faces smashed in . . . after their death. Was it to keep them from feeding on the living?

Frankenstein
Bronze age bodies (2,000–500 BCE) are found cobbled together from six different skeletons in Scotland's bogs.

Neanderthals
Possible Bigfoot ancestor

King Kong
Lives on Skull Island during the Pliocene epoch

I am the largest ape!

Early Wolves (Canis lupus)
Possible werewolf ancestor

Gigantopithecus blacki
The largest ape ever to walk the earth. It may have been Bigfoot's ancestor.

Kraken
Possible prehistoric monster

Plesiosauria
Believed to be the Loch Ness monster

Ichthyosaur
The first "sea monsters" appear.

Godzilla
Hides in his cave

Gorgonopsids
Ferocious and largest predator of the Permian period, 10 feet (3 m)

Estemmenosuchus
Before dinosaurs, these Gargoyle-like, horned creatures were the largest beasts at 10 feet (3 m).

Dunkleosteus
The 19.7-foot (6 m) armored fish terrorized the ocean.

Anomalocaris canadensis
Resemble giant shrimp, have razor-sharp teeth

Trilobites
Distant relatives of insects

Stromatolites
Formed by cyanobacteria. They produce the earth's first oxygen.

Dickinsonia
Oldest creature visible without a microscope

Modern humans appear.

First humans appear. Bigfoot hides in the forest.

An asteroid hits the planet, killing the dinosaurs, but Godzilla survives.

The first dinosaurs appear. They evolved from reptiles.

Big extinction or zombie apocalypse? Nine out of ten species die.

ERA	EPOCH	
CENOZOIC	HOLOCENE	10,000 YEARS AGO
	PLEISTOCENE	1.8
	PLIOCENE	5.3
	MIOCENE	23
	OLIGOCENE	33.9
	EOCENE	55.8
	PALEOCENE	65.5
MESOZOIC	CRETACEOUS	145.5
	JURASSIC	199.6
	TRIASSIC	251
PALEOZOIC	PERMIAN	299
	PENNSYLVANIAN	318
	MISSISSIPPIAN	359.2
	DEVONIAN	419
	SILURIAN	443
	ORDOVICIAN	485.4
	CAMBRIAN	542
	PROTEROZOIC	2.5 BILLION YEARS AGO
	ARCHEAN	4.6 BILLIONS YEARS AGO

THE GEOLOGIC SCALE

A Geologic Time Scale (GTS) dates the history of Earth by matching the fossils trapped in its layers to a particular time frame. Using GTS, a fossil found in a deeper layer of Earth is older than a fossil found closer to the surface. By further examining rocks and fossil records, we can then match which monstrous creatures were living in which era. For example, geologists know that dinosaurs and giant reptiles, like Godzilla, would be found in the Mesozoic era while vampires and werewolves are found in the more recent Cenozoic era. These eras are further broken down into periods, epochs, and ages.

CENOZOIC ERA

At the beginning of the Cenozoic era, a giant asteroid hits present-day Mexico, ending the 165 million-year reign of all non-avian dinosaurs. But the dinosaurs' death leads to new life—mammals. Saber-toothed tigers, giant ground sloths, woolly mammoths and, of course, humans dominate the planet. The first humans (*Homo erectus*) appear during the Pleistocene epoch. About eleven thousand years ago, also during the Pleistocene epoch, the great ice age occurs, and large sections of the planet are blanketed with ice fields and glaciers.

> Uh-oh! Run for cover!

MESOZOIC ERA

During the Permian extinction, Earth transforms into one large supercontinent called Pangea. Ancient plankton deep in the ocean become today's oil. The planet is much warmer now, and a new group dominates the planet—dinosaurs. Some of the deadliest reptiles grow fins and adapt into sea monsters—the ichthyosaur, and possibly the kraken and Godzilla.

PALEOZOIC ERA

Earth is a very different planet during this era. Scorpions the size of dogs and dragonflies the size of hawks roam the planet. Deadly monsters like the Gorgonopsid use razor-sharp teeth to attack prey. But what really makes the earth uninhabitable is not the predators that roam the Siberian plains but the molten lava that erupts from deep inside the earth and the subsequent ash that fills the atmosphere. This falling ash turns most of the oceans pink and strips the water of oxygen. This fiery hellscape leads to the deadliest extinction the planet has ever known, killing over 95 percent of all life. It becomes known as the Permian extinction or the Great Dying. Coal is formed from the plants and animals that died during this mass extinction.

> Not even zombies survived the Permian extinction.

PROTEROZOIC AND ARCHEAN EONS

Meteorites collide and gravity pulls the dust into rocks that form the planet. With temperatures over 2,000°F (1,093°C), Earth resembles a molten hell. There is no free oxygen. There is only carbon dioxide, nitrogen, and water vapor.

WHEN SCIENCE IS WRONG . . .

As a child, I read every book I could find on the "tyrant lizard" monster known as *Tyrannosaurus rex*. I imagined him terrorizing the other puny dinosaurs and arranged my set of plastic dinosaurs with *T. rex* as the leader of the prehistoric pack.

As an adult, I was excited to research the dinosaur that inspired Godzilla but felt duped when I learned my beloved *T. rex* was covered with downy feathers and not scales. How could my ferocious dinosaur look more like a fluffy Big Bird character than a monstrous beast? Still, I wanted to be accurate to *T. rex*'s legacy, so I painstakingly drew each and every feather on my snarling *T. rex*. I hated every minute of it.

Right about the time I was done with his silky plume and had consigned myself to more cherished childhood beliefs crushed under the weight of science, the following headline appeared in my Google Alerts: "T-rex was likely covered in scales, not feathers." In June of 2017, researchers took skin impressions from *T. rex* fossils to prove that they had mostly scales, thereby reversing their prior claim of feathers.

The lesson I learned from all the feathers I erased was this: science can give us answers to our most puzzling questions, but it has the right to change those answers at any time. I have done my best to use the most up-to-date information to give you the science behind the most popular monsters, but I encourage you to do your own research. Please use the following sources in fact-checking. Go to your library, get on the internet, or ask a teacher. Look for the proof in all things, and when you can't find the proof, always leave your mind open to the possibilities.

CARLYN BECCIA

SOURCE NOTES

23 John William Polidori, *The Diary of Dr. John William Polidori, 1816, Relating to Byron, Shelley, Etc.*, ed. William Michael Rossetti (London: Elkin Mathews, 1911), https://archive.org/stream /diaryrelatingtob00poliuoft/diaryrelatingtob00poliuoft_djvu.txt.

23 Allan Massie, *Byron's Travels* (London: Sidgwick and Jackson, 1988), 170.

24 Bram Stoker, *Personal Reminiscences of Henry Irving, Volume 1* (Cambridge: Cambridge University Press, 2013), 366.

24 Bram Stoker, *Dracula* (Westminster, London: Archibald Constable, 1897), 18.

24 David J. Skal, "Something in the Blood, Part 1." *Paris Review* (blog), October 27, 2016, https://www.theparisreview.org/blog/2016/10/27 /something-blood-part-1/.

24 Stoker, *Dracula*, 339.

29 Voltaire, *The Works of Voltaire: A Contemporary Version*, trans. William F. Fleming, vol. 13, *A Philosophical Dictionary* (New York: E. R. Du Mont, 1901), 145.

29 Joseph Sheridan Le Fanu, *Carmilla: A Critical Edition* (Syracuse, NY: Syracuse University Press, 2013), 44.

29 Arifa Akbar, "Fangs for the Memory: A Century of Dracula," Independent (London), April 10, 2012, https://www.independent.co.uk /arts-entertainment/books/features/fangs-for-the-memory-a-century -of-dracula-7628021.html.

41 New World Encyclopedia contributors, "Henry I of England," *New World Encyclopedia*, last modified December 16, 2017, http:// www.newworldencyclopedia.org/p/index.php?title=Henry_I_of _England.

57 Ray Morton, *King Kong: The History of a Movie Icon from Fay Wray to Peter Jackson* (New York: Applause Theatre/Cinema Books, 2005), 31.

60 J. B. S. Haldane, "On Being the Right Size," University of California, Los Angeles, last modified December 19, 2011, https://irl.cs.ucla.edu /papers/right-size.html.

78 Montague Summers, *The Werewolf in Lore and Legend* (Mineola, NY: Dover, 2003), 232.

78 Bill Wasik and Monica Murphy, *Rabid: A Cultural History of the World's Most Diabolical Virus* (New York: Penguin, 2013), 76.

79 Merry Wiesner-Hanks, *The Marvelous Hairy Girls: The Gonzales Sisters and Their Worlds* (New Haven, CT: Yale University Press, 2009), 78.

88 Arthur Fisher, "He Seeks the Giant Squid," Ocean Planet, accessed February 6, 2019, https://seawifs.gsfc.nasa.gov/OCEAN_PLANET /HTML/ps_roper.html.

103 "SUPUESTO YETI (BIGFOOT) GRABADO EN SIBERIA RUSIA 17 FEBRERO 2013 (EXPLICACIÓN)," YouTube video, 6:39, posted by Gabehash, February 17, 2013, https://www.youtube.com/watch?v=sDddzxnxxiM.

103 "SUPUESTO YETI."

118 Paula Hammond, *Atlas of the World's Strangest Animals* (New York: Cavendish Square, 2011), 68.

123 M. William Tsutsui, *Godzilla on My Mind: Fifty Years of the King of Monsters* (New York: Palgrave Macmillan, 2004), 33.

123 David Kalat, *A Critical History and Filmography of Toho's Godzilla Series*, 2nd ed. (Jefferson, NC: McFarland, 2017), 133.

131 Alan E. Waltar, *Radiation and Modern Life: Fulfilling Marie Curie's Dream* (Amherst, NY: Prometheus Books, 2004), 22.

SELECTED BIBLIOGRAPHY

ALL MONSTERS

Amin, Ibrahim S. *The Monster Hunter's Handbook: The Ultimate Guide to Saving Mankind from Vampires, Zombies, Hellhounds, and Other Mythical Beasts*. London: Bloomsbury, 2007.

Asma, Stephen T. *On Monsters: An Unnatural History of Our Worst Fears*. Vancouver, BC: Langara College, 2016.

Gerhard, Ken. *A Menagerie of Mysterious Beasts: Encounters with Cryptid Creatures*. Woodbury, MN: Llewellyn, 2016.

Kaplan, Matt. *The Science of Monsters: The Origins of the Creatures We Love to Fear*. New York: Scribner, 2014.

Milano, Roy. *Monsters: A Celebration of the Classics from Universal Studios*. New York: Del Rey, 2006.

Neibaur, James L. *The Monster Movies of Universal Studios*. Lanham, MD: Rowman and Littlefield, 2017.

Storm, Rory. *Monster Hunt: The Guide to Cryptozoology*. New York: Metro Books, 2008.

Van Duzer, Chet A. *Sea Monsters on Medieval and Renaissance Maps*. London: British Library, 2014.

Ventura, Varla. *Banshees, Werewolves, Vampires, and Other Creatures of the Night: Facts, Fictions, and First-Hand Accounts*. San Francisco: Weiser, 2013.

BIGFOOT

Bigfoot Evidence. YouTube channel. Accessed March 6, 2019. https://www.youtube.com/user /BigfootEvidence.

Brockenbrough, Martha. *Finding Bigfoot: Everything You Need to Know*. New York: Feiwel and Friends, 2013.

Colyer, Daryl G., Alton Higgins, Brian Brown, Kathy Strain, Michael C. Mayes, and Brad McAndrews.

The Ouachita Project. Belton, TX: North American Wood Ape Conservancy, 2015. http:// media.texasbigfoot.com/OP_paper_media /OuachitaProjectMonograph_Version1.1 _03112015.pdf.

Daegling, David J. *Bigfoot Exposed: An Anthropologist Examines America's Enduring Legend*. Lanham, MD: Rowman and Littlefield, 2004.

Harari, Yuval Noah. *Sapiens: A Brief History of Humankind*. New York: HarperCollins, 2017.

Horns, Joshua, Rebekah Jung, and David R. Carrier. "*In vitro* Strain in Human Metacarpal Bones during Striking: Testing the Pugilism Hypothesis of Hominin Hand Evolution." *Journal of Experimental Biology*, no. 218 (2015): 3215–3221. https://doi.org/10.1242/jeb.125831.

Loxton, Daniel, and Donald R. Prothero. *Abominable Science: Origins of the Yeti, Nessie, and Other Famous Cryptids*. Chichester, NY: Columbia University Press, 2012.

Meldrum, Jeff. *Sasquatch Field Guide*. Blue Lake, CA: Paradise Cay, 2013.

———. *Sasquatch: Legend Meets Science*. New York: Forge, 2007.

"SUPUESTO YETI (BIGFOOT) GRABADO EN SIBERIA RUSIA 17 FEBRERO 2013 (EXPLICACIÓN)." YouTube video, 6:39. Posted by Gabehash. February 17, 2013. https://www .youtube.com/watch?v=sDddzxnxxiM.

Sykes, Bryan. *Bigfoot, Yeti, and the Last Neanderthal: A Geneticist's Search for Modern Apemen*. Newburyport, MA: Disinformation Books, 2016.

———. *The Nature of the Beast: The First Genetic Evidence on the Survival of Apemen, Yeti, Bigfoot and Other Mysterious Creatures into Modern Times*. London: Coronet, 2014.

DRACULA

Barber, Paul. *Vampires, Burial, and Death: Folklore and Reality*. New Haven, CT: Yale University Press, 2010.

Dix, Jay, and Michael Graham. *Time of Death, Decomposition and Identification: An Atlas*. Causes of Death Atlas series. Boca Raton, FL: CRC, 2017.

Dundes, Alan. *The Vampire: A Casebook*. Madison: University of Wisconsin Press, 1998.

Emery, Kathryn Myers. "New Morbid Terminology: Cadaveric Spasm." *Bones Don't Lie* (blog), October 1, 2013. https://bonesdontlie.wordpress .com/2013/10/01/new-morbid-terminology -cadaveric-spasm/.

Ghose, Tia. "Mystery of 'Vampire' Burials Solved." Live Science, November 26, 2014. https://www .livescience.com/48924-mystery-of-vampire -burials-solved.html.

Jenkins, Mark Collins. *Vampire Forensics: Uncovering the Origins of an Enduring Legend*. Washington, DC: National Geographic, 2011.

Kong, Nikki R. "Chasing Immortality." *Berkeley Science Review*, April 22, 2013. http:// berkeleysciencereview.com/article/chasing -immortality/.

Lecouteux, Claude. *The Secret History of Vampires: Their Multiple Forms and Hidden Purposes*. Rochester, VT: Inner Traditions, 2010.

McClelland, Bruce A. *Slayers and Their Vampires: A Cultural History of Killing the Dead*. Ann Arbor: University of Michigan Press, 2006.

Patel, Samir S. "Plague Vampire Exorcism." Archaeology. Accessed March 6, 2019. http:// archive.archaeology.org/online/features /halloween/plague.html.

Ramsland, Katherine. *The Science of Vampires*. New York: Berkley Boulevard Books, 2002.

Shay, Jerry, and Woodring Wright. "Facts about Telomeres and Telomerase." Shay/Wright Lab, UT Southwestern Medical Center. Accessed February 6, 2019. http://www.utsouthwestern.edu/labs /shay-wright/research/facts-about-telomeres -telomerase.html.

Skal, David J. *Hollywood Gothic: The Tangled Web of Dracula from Novel to Stage to Screen*. New York: Farrar, Straus and Giroux, 2004.

———. *Something in the Blood: The Untold Story of Bram Stoker, the Man Who Wrote Dracula*. New York: Liveright, 2017.

Stoker, Bram. *Dracula*. Westminster, London: Archibald Constable, 1897.

———. *Personal Reminiscences of Henry Irving, Volume 1*. Cambridge: Cambridge University Press, 2013.

Sugg, Richard. *Mummies, Cannibals, and Vampires: The History of Corpse Medicine from the Renaissance to the Victorians*, 2nd ed. London: Routledge, 2015

FRANKENSTEIN
Anthes, Emily. *Frankenstein's Cat: Cuddling Up to Biotech's Brave New Beasts*. New York: Scientific American/Farrar, Straus and Giroux, 2013.

Ashcroft, Frances. *The Spark of Life: Electricity in the Human Body*. New York: Norton, 2013.

Elsenaar, Arthur, and Remko Scha. "Electric Body Manipulation as Performance Art: A Historical Perspective." *Leonardo Music Journal* 12 (2002): 17–28. http://www.leonardo.info/isast/articles /else.scha.pdf.

Fara, Patricia. *An Entertainment for Angels: Electricity in the Enlightenment*. Cambridge, UK: Icon, 2002.

Hitchcock, Susan Tyler. *Frankenstein: A Cultural History*. New York: W. W. Norton, 2007.

Hoobler, Dorothy, and Thomas Hoobler. *The Monsters: Mary Shelley and the Curse of Frankenstein*. New York: Little, Brown, 2006.

Johnson, Jessica P. "Animal Electricity, circa 1781." *Scientist*, September 28, 2011. http://www.the-scientist.com/?articles.view/ articleNo/31078/title/Animal-Electricity-- circa-1781/.

Lederer, Susan. *Frankenstein: Penetrating the Secrets of Nature*. New Brunswick, NJ: Rutgers University Press, 2002.

Magnet Academy. "Luigi Galvani." National High Magnetic Field Laboratory. Accessed February 1, 2019. https://nationalmaglab.org/education /magnet-academy/history-of-electricity-magnetism /pioneers/luigi-galvani.

Massie, Allan. *Byron's Travels*. London: Sidgwick and Jackson, 1988.

Montillo, Roseanne. *The Lady and Her Monsters: A Tale of Dissections, Real-Life Dr. Frankensteins, and the Creation of Mary Shelley's Masterpiece*. New York: William Morrow, 2013.

Piccolino, Marco. "Luigi Galvani and Animal Electricity: Two Centuries after the Foundation of Electrophysiology." *Trends Neurosci* 20, no. 10 (October 1997): 443–448. https://doi.org /10.1016/S0166-2236(97)01101-6.

GODZILLA
American Osteopathic College of Occupational and Preventative Medicine. "Ionizing and Non-Ionizing Radiation Study Guide." Basic Course III Orlando, October 31, 2011. http://www.aocopm .org/assets/documents/10-31-11_Basic _Course_III_Orlando/ionizing%20an%20non.pdf.

AtomicBombMuseum.org. "Destructive Effects." Accessed March 6, 2019. http://atomicbombmuseum .org/3_health.shtml.

Brothers, H. Peters. *Atomic Dreams and the Nuclear Nightmare: The Making of Godzilla*. Seattle: Createspace Books, 2015.

Centers for Disease Control and Prevention. "Radioactive Contamination and Radiation Exposure." Center for Preparedness and Response. Last modified October 10, 2014. https://emergency.cdc.gov/radiation /contamination.asp.

Christiansen, Per. "Godzilla from a Zoological Perspective." *Mathematical Geology* 32, no. 2 (February 2000): 231–245. https://doi.org /10.1023/A:1007531524040.

Compton, Karl T. "If the Atomic Bomb Had Not Been Used: Was Japan Already Beaten before the August 1945 Bombings?" *Atlantic*, December 1946. https://www.theatlantic.com/magazine /archive/1946/12/if-the-atomic-bomb-had-not -been-used/376238/.

Greshko, Michael. "Hiroshima's Radiation." *Inside Science*. Accessed March 6, 2019. https://www .insidescience.org/sites/default/files/hiroshima -radiation.pdf.

Groeger, Lena. "Radiation Levels Explained." *Scientific American*. Accessed February 6, 2019. https://www.scientificamerican.com/media/inline /blog/Image/RadiationExplainerFINAL4.jpg.

Kalat, David. *A Critical History and Filmography of Toho's Godzilla Series*. 2nd ed. Jefferson, NC: McFarland, 2017.

Lee, Brianna. "How Much Radiation Is Too Much? A Handy Guide." *Daily Need* (blog), *PBS*, March 22, 2011. http://www.pbs.org/wnet/need-to-know /the-daily-need/how-much-radiation-is-too-much -a-handy-guide/8124/.

McCandless, David, and Matt Hancock. "Radiation Dosage Chart." Version 2.02. Information Is Beautiful. Last modified August 2013. http://www.informationisbeautiful.net /visualizations/radiation-dosage-chart/.

Naish, Darren. "The Science of Godzilla." *Tetrapod Zoology* (blog), February 7, 2007. http://scienceblogs.com/tetrapodzoology/2007/02/07/the-science-of-godzilla-1/.

National Aeronautics and Space Administration, Goddard Space Flight Center. "The Electromagnetic Spectrum." Imagine the Universe! Last modified March 2013. https://imagine.gsfc.nasa.gov/science/toolbox/emspectrum1.html.

Sara, Sally. "Hiroshima Bombing Survivor Tomiko Matsumoto: A Message of Peace from a Survivor of Hell." *Australian Broadcasting Corporation* (Sydney), June 14, 2015. http://www.abc.net.au/news/specials/mama-asia/2015-06-15/hiroshima-bomb-survivor-tomiko-matsumoto/5486678.

Theerakulstit, Shyaporn. "Godzilla: History, Biology and Behavior of Hyper-Evolved Theropod Kaiju." *Smithsonian Magazine* video, 19:39. Accessed March 6, 2019. http://www.smithsonianmag.com/videos/category/future-is-here/godzilla-history-biology-and-behavior-of-h/.

Tsutsui, M. William. *Godzilla on My Mind: Fifty Years of the King of Monsters*. New York: Palgrave Macmillan, 2004.

Venton, Danielle. "The Impossible Anatomy of Godzilla." *Popular Mechanics*, May 14, 2014. http://www.popularmechanics.com/culture/movies/a10476/the-impossible-anatomy-of-godzilla-16785535/.

Wells, Pamela Caragol, and Holly Taylor. *24 Hours after Hiroshima*, DVD. Directed by Pamela Caragol Wells. Los Angeles: 20th Century Fox, 2010.

World Nuclear Association. "Nuclear Radiation and Health Effects." Information Library. Last modified June 2018. http://www.world-nuclear.org/information-library/safety-and-security/radiation-and-health/nuclear-radiation-and-health-effects.aspx.

———. "Radiation and Radioactivity." Accessed February 6, 2019. http://www.world-nuclear.org/uploadedFiles/org/Features/Radiation/Radiation_Collected.pdf.

KING KONG

Ewalt, David M. "The Biology of King Kong." *Forbes*, December 12, 2005. https://www.forbes.com/2005/12/12/king-kong-biology_cx_de_1213kongbiology.html.

Ghose, Tia. "Gorillas Use Stinky B.O. to Say 'Back Off.'" Live Science, July 9, 2014. http://www.livescience.com/46719-gorillas-use-smell-communication.html.

Lucas. "8 Prehistoric Animals That Were Ever Dominating the World." Enki Village. Accessed February 6, 2019. http://www.enki-village.com/prehistoric-animals.html.

Morton, Ray. *King Kong: The History of a Movie Icon from Fay Wray to Peter Jackson*. New York: Applause Theatre/Cinema Books, 2005.

Rastogi, Nina Shen. "A Snake the Size of a Plane: How Did Prehistoric Animals Get So Big?" Slate, February 5, 2009. http://www.slate.com/articles/news_and_politics/explainer/2009/02/a_snake_the_size_of_a_plane.html.

Simmons, Charles. "Tigra Scientifica: Death of the Hobbits." *Tiger* (Clemson Univerity, SC), February 13, 2017. http://www.thetigernews.com/news/tigra-scientifica-death-of-the-hobbits/article_b9dd1a14-f192-11e6-a8fd-3f0c4b5bd1e4.html.

Strauss, Mark. "The Largest Ape That Ever Lived Was Doomed by Its Size: The Demise of *Gigantopithecus* Some 100,000 Years Ago Reveals Why Big Is Often Not Better." *National Geographic*, January 5, 2016. http://news.nationalgeographic.com/2016/01/160106-science-evolution-apes-giant/.

Tyson, Peter. "Gigantism and Dwarfism on Islands." *NOVA, PBS*, October 31, 2000. http://www.pbs.org/wgbh/nova/evolution/gigantism-and-dwarfism-islands.html.

Wake, Jenny. *The Making of King Kong: The Official Guide to the Motion Picture*. New York: Pocket Books, 2005.

"Why Do Gorillas Pound Their Chest?" YouTube video, 2:13. Posted by Animalist, May 29, 2014. https://www.youtube.com/watch?v=yoxVlKoQ1cg.

THE KRAKEN

Babington, Charles C., John Edward Gray, William S. Dallas, and William Francis. *The Annals and Magazine of Natural History: Including Zoology, Botany, and Geology*. Series 4, Vol. 13, London: Taylor and Francis, 1874.

Ellis, Richard. *The Search for the Giant Squid*. London: Robert Hale, 1999.

Hamilton, Robert. *The Naturalist's Library*. Vol. 25, *Mammalia*. Edited by William Jardine. London: Chatto and Windus, 1839. http://www.biodiversitylibrary.org/item/60177#page/391/mode/1up.

Hopkins, Michael. "Giant Squid Snapped in the Deep: World's Largest Invertebrate Is Caught on Camera for First Time." *Nature*, September 28, 2005. https:// doi.org/10.1038/news050926-7.

"Live Giant Squid Caught on Camera." *BBC News*, September 28, 2005. http://news.bbc.co.uk/2/hi/science/nature/4288772.stm.

Martin, Myrna. "Oceanic Zones." Kids Fun Science. Accessed March 6, 2019. http://www.kids-fun-science.com/oceanic-zones.html.

McClain, Craig R., Meghan A. Balk, Mark C. Benfield, Trevor A. Branch, Catherine Chen, James Cosgrove, Alistair D. M. Dove et al. "Sizing Ocean Giants: Patterns of Intraspecific Size Variation in Marine Megafauna." *PeerJ* 3 (January 2015): 715. https://doi.org/10.7717/peerj.715.

New Zealand Te Papa Tongarewa. "The Colossal Squid Exhibition-Anatomy-Interactive." Colossal Squid. Accessed February 6, 2019. http://squid.tepapa.govt.nz/anatomy/interactive.

Staaf, Danna. *Squid Empire: The Rise and Fall of the Cephalopods*. Lebanon, NH: University Press of New England/ForeEdge, 2017.

Widder, Edith. "How We Found the Giant Squid." Filmed at TED2013, February 2013. Long Beach, CA. Video, 8:31. https://www.ted.com/talks /edith_widder_how_we_found_the_giant_squid /transcript?language=en.

Williams, Wendy. *Kraken: The Curious, Exciting, and Slightly Disturbing Science of Squid*. New York: Abrams, 2011.

WEREWOLVES

Baring-Gould, Sabine. *Book of Werewolves: Being an Account of a Terrible Superstition*. London: Forgotten Books, 2015.

Linnell, John D. C., Reidar Andersen, Zanete Andersone, Linas Balciauskas, Juan Carlos Blanco, Luigi Boitani, Scott Brainerd et al. "The Fear of Wolves: A Review of Wolf Attacks on Humans." Norsk institutt for naturforskning, January 2002. http://digitalcommons.unl.edu /cgi/viewcontent.cgi?article=1026&context =wolfrecovery.

McAllister, Peter. *Manthropology: The Science of Why the Modern Male Is Not the Man He Used to Be*. New York: St. Martin's, 2013.

Parade. *The Secret World of Cats and Dogs: Inside the Minds of Our Best Friends*. Parade special edition. Athlon #12, 2016.

Renfield, R. K. *Meet the Wolfman*. New York: Rosen, 2005.

Sánchez Romero, Gustavo, and S. R. Schwalb. *Beast: Werewolves, Serial Killers, and Man-Eaters; The Mystery of the Monsters of the Gévaudan*. New York: Skyhorse, 2016.

Sidky, Homayun. *Witchcraft, Lycanthropy, Drugs, and Disease: An Anthropological Study of the European Witch-Hunts*. New York: Peter Lang, 2004.

Smithsonian Channel. *The Real Beauty and the Beast*. Directed by Julian Roman Poelsler. Washington, DC: Smithsonian Channel, 2014.

Steiger, Brad. *The Werewolf Book: The Encyclopedia of Shape-Shifting Beings*. Canton, MI: Visible Ink, 2012.

Summers, Montague. *The Werewolf in Lore and Legend*. Mineola, NY: Dover, 2003.

Tng, Vivian E. T., and Sally de Zwaan. "Hypertrichosis Cubiti: A Case Report and Literature Review." *Clinical Case Reports* 4, no. 2 (December 2015): 138–142. https://doi .org/10.1002/ccr3.465.

Wasik, Bill, and Monica Murphy. *Rabid: A Cultural History of the World's Most Diabolical Virus*. New York: Penguin, 2013.

Wiesner-Hanks, Merry. *The Marvelous Hairy Girls: The Gonzales Sisters and Their Worlds*. New Haven, CT: Yale University Press, 2009.

ZOMBIES

Bates, Mary. "Meet 5 'Zombie' Parasites That Mind-Control Their Hosts." *National Geographic*, October 22, 2018. http://news.nationalgeographic .com/news/2014/10/141031-zombies-parasites -animals-science-halloween/.

Bishop, Kyle William. *American Zombie Gothic: The Rise and Fall (and Rise) of the Walking Dead in Popular Culture*. Jefferson, NC: McFarland, 2010.

Brooks, Max. *The Zombie Survival Guide: Complete Protection from the Living Dead*. New York: Three Rivers, 2003.

Center for Preparedness and Response. "Zombie Preparedness Products." Centers for Disease Control and Prevention. Accessed March 6, 2019. https://www.cdc.gov/cpr/zombie/index.htm.

Cole, James. "Assessing the Calorific Significance of Episodes of Human Cannibalism in the Palaeolithic. *Scientific Reports* 7 (2017). https:// www.nature.com/articles/srep44707.

Kielpinski, Gerald, and Brian Gleisberg. *Surviving the Zombie Outbreak: The Official Zombie Survival Field Manual*. Valencia, CA: Guffaw, 2011.

Malik, Kenan. *Man, Beast, and Zombie: What Science Can and Cannot Tell Us about Human Nature*. New Brunswick, NJ: Rutgers University Press, 2002.

Munz, Philip, Ioan Hudea, Joe Imad, and Robert J. Smith. "When Zombies Attack! Mathematical Modelling of an Outbreak of Zombie Infection." Loe.org, November 21, 2008. http://loe.org /images/content/091023/Zombie%20Publication .pdf.

Verstynen, Timothy, and Bradley Voytek. *Do Zombies Dream of Undead Sheep? A Neuroscientific View of the Zombie Brain*. Princeton, NJ: Princeton University Press, 2016.

Wanjek, Christopher, Live Science. "Rage Disorder Linked with Parasite Found in Cat Feces." *Scientific American*, March 26, 2016. http://www .scientificamerican.com/article/rage-disorder -linked-with-parasite-found-in-cat-feces/.

Worobey, Michael. "The Genesis of the 1918 Spanish Influenza Pandemic." YouTube video, 1:08:08. Posted by the University of Arizona, May 1, 2014. https://www. youtube.com/watch?v=48Klc3DPdtk.

GLOSSARY

ambergris: a waxy block that sperm whales vomit up when they can't digest something. It is sometimes used in perfume and can be very valuable.

ambush hunter: an animal that hides and waits for its prey to come to it before attacking

amygdala: an almond-shaped part of the brain that controls emotions and triggers the fight-or-flight response

atom: a microscopic piece of matter containing protons, neutrons, and electrons

basal ganglia: the part of the brain controlling basic movement and the learning of new movements

bioluminescence: the ability of living things to create their own light

brain stem: the area at the base of the brain that connects to the spinal cord. It is responsible for involuntary functions like breathing, swallowing, and the heart beating.

Broca's area: an area in the front-left part of the brain that controls speech and language comprehension

cannibalism: eating members of one's own species, particularly humans eating other humans

cephalopod: a group of marine mollusks that includes squid, cuttlefish, clams, and octopuses

cerebellum: the lower back part of the brain responsible for coordinating muscle movement, including balance, speech, and posture

coccyx: the scientific term for the tailbone, or the remaining part of the tail that humans had in the womb

conductor: a material that lets electricity flow through it because it can easily gain or lose electrons

cryptid: an animal whose existence has not been verified by scientists

decomposition: the natural process of a body breaking down after death

defibrillator: a medical device that provides an electric current to the heart to restore its normal rhythm

deviant burial: a burial different from the typical burial ritual of the period or region

dopamine: a neurotransmitter, or chemical messenger, that sends signals to the brain when a person feels pleasure—or fear

electric current: the movement or flow of electricity from one place to another

electron: a particle within an atom that is negatively charged and forms a cloud surrounding the nucleus

epidemic: an outbreak of disease that spreads rapidly and infects whole communities

fight-or-flight response: a basic survival instinct triggered by the amygdala that creates a surge of energy, sharpened senses, and a fast pulse to help people attack or run from an enemy

fusiform face area: the region of the brain that identifies human faces

hippocampus: the region of the brain that controls long-term memory and emotion

hypertrichosis: also known as werewolf syndrome, this condition causes people to grow thick hair on parts of the body that don't usually have much hair

hypothalamus: the region of the brain that controls body temperature, thirst, hunger, sleep, and other basic needs

incubation period: the time period between catching an infection and showing symptoms of it

insular dwarfism: an evolutionary process by which large animals stranded on an island become smaller to better match their environments

insular gigantism: an evolutionary process by which small animals stranded on an island become larger to better match their environments

insulator: material that makes it difficult for electricity to flow through it because it doesn't easily gain or lose electrons

ionizing radiation: a form of short wavelength radiation that can break molecular bonds and remove electrons from atoms or molecules when it passes through air, water, or living things. The removal of electrons may lead to changes in living cells.

keloid scar: a large, bumpy section of scar tissue that forms after a serious injury or nuclear attack

keratin: the fibrous protein that makes up hair, nails, and skin

kuru: a rare disease caused by eating dead human brain tissue that contains the infectious protein prion

lanugo: soft, downy hair that covers babies in the womb and sometimes shortly after birth

lycanthropy: transforming from human to wolf or having a mental illness that creates delusions of being a wolf

microbiome: the microorganisms that live inside an organism and help with functions like digestion

neutron: a particle within the nucleus of an atom that has no electrical charge

nuclear fallout: the toxic radioactive material that falls from the sky after a nuclear explosion

nucleus: the center of an atom containing protons and neutrons

olfactory bulb: the part of the brain that detects and interprets smells

osteoderms: bony plates or scales on an animal that form a protective shield

pandemic: an outbreak of disease that rapidly spreads throughout the world

photosynthesis: the process plants use to turn sunlight into food and energy

placebo effect: a medical phenomenon in which people who are given a fake treatment for an illness actually feel better because of it

prefrontal cortex: the part of the brain that acts as a control center for the rest of the brain, making decisions and planning what to do next

prion: an abnormal prion protein that progressively harms the brain. Several infectious diseases, including kuru, are caused by consuming infected brain tissue.

proton: a particle within the nucleus of an atom that has a positive electrical charge

purge fluid: a reddish-brown fluid that leaks out of the body through the mouth after death

rete mirabile: a network of flexible blood vessels that controls how much blood can get to the brain, acting like a sponge to collect the extra blood flowing to the head

revenant: the term for a vampire or reanimated corpse from the fifteenth to the seventeenth centuries

senescence: the last stage of life (old age) when cells can no longer divide

skin slippage: a decomposition process in which the outer layers of skin loosen and break, revealing the layers of skin underneath and making it appear as though the corpse has grown new skin

species: a group of organisms that can produce fertile offspring

square-cube law: a mathematical principle that describes the relationship between a shape's (or a monster's) surface area and volume as the shape changes size. As size increases, volume increases faster than surface area.

static electricity: electricity that builds up on surfaces when different types of objects touch and transfer electrons

stop-motion animation: a kind of filmmaking in which objects are photographed repeatedly, with the animators moving the objects slightly between photos. When the photos are played back fast enough, they create the illusion of movement.

takotsubo cardiomyopathy: a heart condition in which the left ventricle balloons out and weakens, creating symptoms similar to a heart attack. The condition almost exclusively affects older women and is named for the Japanese *takotsubo* jar used to catch octopus. It is also called broken heart syndrome.

telomerase: an enzyme that protects telomeres from getting shortened, lessening or avoiding the impact of the aging process

telomere: a small cap at the end of a chromosome that keeps DNA from becoming damaged and prevents mistakes when cells divide. Telomeres shorten over time and eventually stop the body from creating new cells.

thalamus: the middle part of the brain that interprets signals from different body parts and turns them into the senses

volume: the amount of space an object or organism occupies

INDEX

aging, 19
  reversing, 38–39
ambush hunters, 72–73, 98
ancestors, 72
  ape, 64–66, 107–108
  human, 6–7, 51, 73, 106–107, 110–111
atomic bomb, 121–123, 130–133
atoms, 9, 96, 130
  parts of, 9, 14, 16, 130

bacteria, 25–27, 37, 48
Bigfoot, 103–119
  attacks, 117
  infographic, 113
  other names for, 103
  theories, 106–109
  timeline, 104–105
  tracking, 112–116
blood, 4, 7, 19, 23–30, 33–34, 40–41, 52, 59, 78, 88–89, 121, 124–125, 129
  drinking, 32–34
  loss of, 36–37
books
  Carmilla, 29
  Dracula, 23, 28–31, 34, 41
  Frankenstein, 12–13, 21, 23
  Interview with a Vampire, 31
  Moby Dick, 97
  Modern Prometheus, The, 13
  One Flew over the Cuckoo's Nest, 20
  Twilight Saga, 31
  Vampyre, The, 23, 29
brain, 6–8, 15, 21, 32–33, 36, 39, 44–45, 50–52, 54–55, 88–89, 119, 124–126, 136
  parts of the, 6–8, 14–15, 44–45

cannibalism, 51, 80
cells, 15, 34–35, 38–39, 44, 46, 48, 89, 128–129
cryptids, 109, 118–119

decomposition, 26–27, 29, 37, 45, 48–49
Dracula, Vlad, 23–24, 28

electricity, 9–12, 14–17, 53
  electric current, 9–11, 14–17
  experiments with, 10–11, 16–17
  history of, 9, 16
  static electricity, 9–10, 16

emergency kit, 53, 134
evolution, 41, 64–65, 72–73, 106–107, 127
  skull, 110–111

fear, 5–7, 18, 21, 24–26, 28, 45, 69, 75–76, 80, 83, 99, 103, 117, 131, 133, 136
flatline, 15
Frankenstein, 9–21
  infographic, 18
  machine, 9, 14–15
  monster, 9, 18, 21
  movies, 13–14, 17–18, 21, 30
  novel, 12–13, 21, 23
  scientist, 9, 12, 20–21

genetic engineering, 13, 18, 41, 46
Godzilla, 59, 94, 121–137
  fallout, 121–123, 133–134
  infographics, 129, 134–135
  movies, 121, 123–125, 131
  radiation, 121–123, 126, 130–135

infographics
  are you stronger than a dung beetle?, 62–63
  best states to find Bigfoot, 113
  holding your breath, 129
  how to survive Godzilla's nuclear breath, 134–135
  Kraken size comparison, 90
  spider goats, 18
  states you are most likely to be eaten by a zombie, 47
  that's bananas, 61
  undead or dead?, 27
  where to find the Kraken and other sea creatures, 94
  which beast kills the most people?, 77
  zombie virus life cycle, 49

King Kong, 57–67, 123–125
  Giganto, 61, 107–108
  infographics, 61, 62–63
  island rule, 64–65
  movies, 57–58, 60, 64–67
  square-cube law, 58–60, 62

Kraken, 7, 85–101
  ambergris, 86–87
  catching a, 98–99
  cephalopods, 88, 92
  deep-sea gigantism, 100–101
  density and a, 96–97
  infographics, 90, 94
  theories, 88–92

monsters, 17, 18, 25, 28, 58–59, 79, 80, 118–119, 125
  real, 20–21, 40–41, 54–55, 82–83, 100–101, 136–137
movies
  Dracula, 30–31
  Frankenstein, 13–14, 17–18, 21, 30
  Godzilla, 121, 123–125, 131
  Horror of Dracula, 30
  Interview with a Vampire, 31
  King Kong, 57–58, 60, 64–67
  Lost Boys, The, 31
  Night of the Living Dead, 48
  Nosferatu, 30
  Titanic, 95
  Twilight Series, 31
  vampire, 34, 38
  White Zombie, 43
  zombie, 46, 52, 54

pandemics, 48–49
  Bubonic Plague, 25, 28, 46, 48
  Great Influenza, 46
plague, 25, 28, 46

rabies, 40, 46, 48, 80
radiation
  animals affected by, 136–137
  Marie Curie and, 131
  Godzilla and, 121–123, 126, 130–135

revenants, 28
  burial of, 25

science, 6–7, 35, 96–97, 100, 106, 109, 127
  death, 25–27, 38–39
  ethics and, 13, 18–21
  magic of, 4–5
  new, 9, 41, 110–111, 131, 140
  placebo effect, 72

scientists
  Curie, Marie, 131
  Galvani, Luigi, 10–11, 15–16
  Landsteiner, Karl, 35
  mad, 20–21
shape-shifters, 69, 82–83
square-cube law, 58–60, 62, 125

telomeres, 38–39
transgenesis, 18

vampires, 23–41
  animal, 40–41
  attacks, 36–37
  biting, 32–33
  infographic, 27
  killing, 24–25
  movies, 30–31, 34, 38
  novels, 23–24, 28–31
  timeline, 28–31
viruses, 25, 80
  blood, 41
  zombie, 46–49, 51

werewolves, 69–83
  attacks, 76–77
  hypertrichosis, 79
  infographic, 77
  lycanthropy, 69, 78
  movies, 69, 72
witches, 28, 43, 69, 73
writers
  Byron, Lord George Gordon, 12, 23, 29
  Kesey, Ken, 20
  Melville, Herman, 97
  Meyer, Stephanie, 31
  Polidori, John, 23, 29
  Rice, Anne, 31
  Seabrook, William, 43
  Shelley, Mary, 12–13, 23
  Sheridan le Fanu, Joseph, 29
  Stoker, Bram, 23–24, 28–31

zombies, 7, 14, 27, 43–55
  animal, 54–55
  healthy, 50–51
  infographics, 47, 49
  movies, 43, 46, 48, 54
  preparedness kit, 53, 134
  voodoo and, 43

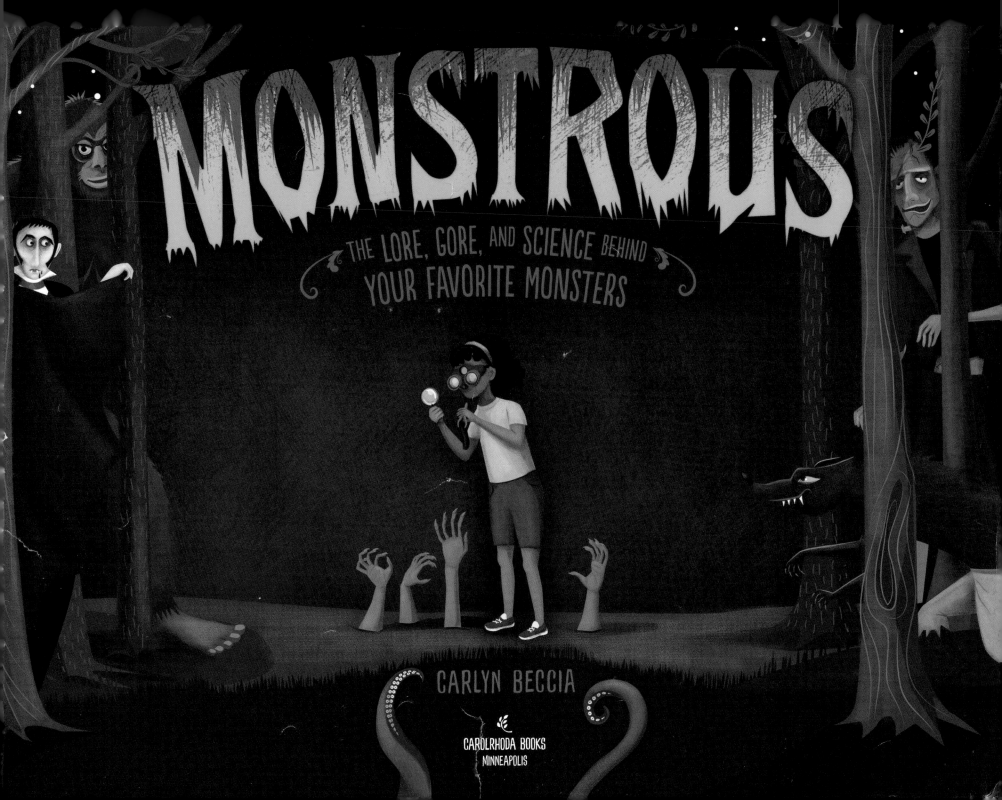

MONSTROUS

THE LORE, GORE, AND SCIENCE BEHIND
YOUR FAVORITE MONSTERS

CARLYN BECCIA

CAROLRHODA BOOKS

MINNEAPOLIS